ELEGANT DECORATING
ON A LIMITED BUDGET

ELEGANT DECORATING ON A LIMITED BUDGET

Have an Attractive Setting Now and
Quality Pieces for the Future

BY JANET ASTON REIST

THE MACMILLAN COMPANY, NEW YORK
COLLIER-MACMILLAN LIMITED, LONDON

THIRD PRINTING 1966

The Macmillan Company, New York

Collier-Macmillan Canada Ltd., Toronto, Ontario

Library of Congress catalog card number: 65-17822

Printed in the United States of America

To My Family—

The most important part of my decorating scheme

ACKNOWLEDGMENTS

MY thanks go to Carol Mohnkern, Jeanne Ahearn, and Elizabeth Peel who, because of our frequent moves, all became involved in typing this manuscript; to Henry Friedman of Lexington, Mass., and William Martinez of Pittsburgh, Pa., for their fine photographs; to the Robert Vesses of Pittsburgh, Pa., for their patience and cooperation while some of these photographs were done in their delightful house; to the antique dealers who taught me much of what I know about antiques, particularly Gerald Patton of Duncansville, Pa., and Grace Barker of State College, Pa.; to the cabinet makers who have let me in on many of their secrets, principally John Hartzler of Belleville, Pa., and Bronnie Warsaskas of Arlington, Mass.; to my friends and family, who provided suggestions, ideas, and encouragement, and most especially to my husband who helped me in *every* phase of the research and preparation of this book.

CONTENTS

INTRODUCTION

HAVE you ever, with great anticipation, opened a "home" magazine that promised you "glamour on a budget" or something equally enticing, only to find that the so-called "budget" was geared to the income of a Rockefeller heir? Or have you ever rushed home from the book store to digest a book on decorating and been disappointed because the author had far too elaborate ideas for your limited time, money, and resources? Oh sure, you've probably read articles about how you can make "cute little items" from orange crates, but these don't have much appeal when you want to collect quality pieces from the start. These, among others, were the problems which faced me as a bride six years ago, and those which I have heard many of my friends complain about ever since.

Many professionals in the Interior Design field, with their exposure to the elaborate, appear to have lost touch with the problems which plague us. This is frustrating, to say the least, since it is in the beginning, when funds are short and the whole concept of decorating is new, that one needs help. That is why I thought a book written by one who has recently been through this initial period—and is keenly aware of its problems—would be helpful.

My early problems in decorating and housekeeping were fairly typical—a student husband, a working me, little money (but big ideas), many moves and much informal entertaining —and on my small budget I wanted to begin working toward elegant rooms with quality furniture, not a collection of inexpensive makeshifts. I hope that my observations through this period will be of some value to those of you who are just starting.

Long-range planning is one of the keys to successful decorating and much of this planning is dependent on certain attitudes. Therefore, I have gone into the basic philosophies which I feel lead to elegant, but inexpensive, decorating with an individual flair as well as those which can be one's downfall.

From there I go on to a discussion of colors and period styles—two subjects imperative for an understanding of good decorating.

True, much has been written about these, but besides giving a few suggestions, I have tried to show how you can acquire a "feel" for color rather than giving any rules for it. And as for period furniture, besides discussing its importance, atmosphere, and uses, I have included outlines which give a concise chronological run down, together with atmosphere and attributes, of the important periods from the early Renaissance (fifteenth century) to the twentieth century.

These outlines are brief and you will want to investigate the individual periods at much greater length—especially those which particularly interest you—but I hope they will serve as an introduction and a ready reference. I know how frustrating it is to have to pore over several volumes and much of the world's history in order to find out just where "Directoire" furniture fits into the picture. Though, incidentally, one does learn an incredible amount of history, quite painlessly, through study of furniture styles. Period furniture evolved quite logically out of the times, and in doing these outlines much history came alive and fell beautifully into place for me. They were great fun to do and I hope you will enjoy them.

I have dealt with these general discussions before going on to more specific subjects since one needs some basic premises before fully appreciating individual suggestions.

It is not much help for a book or magazine to say blithely, "Wing chairs are back; try one in your living room—in red maybe!" or "Here's how to refinish that Victorian side chair of yours" if, first, you don't know what you are working toward; second, you haven't thought much about colors and the suggestion of bright red sends you into panic, and third, how in heaven's name will it fit in with all your French provincial furniture? As for a Victorian side chair—what's that?

You must first have some understanding of decorating and know what you are trying to accomplish. This leads to a feeling of confidence that lets you discern which ideas you can use for inspiration and interpret into your own individual decorating scheme, and which ones should be rejected as not for you. Then you are not thrown constantly into a quandary of indecision.

I hope the chapters with specific suggestions will yield some ideas which will appeal to you and which you can work into your plan.

Decorating is one of the things that makes the job of housekeeping truly creative (I always feel a bit sorry for the woman who, when asked her profession, replies apologetically, "just a housewife"), and it is this creativity which makes homemaking rewarding and fun. But, when this creativity is stifled by such frustration as lack of money, not knowing where to start, or a rash and disappointing purchase, decorating and housekeeping often become drudgery. Therefore, it is very important to get off to a good start with your decorating. I have tried to discuss how you can have attractive surroundings from the beginning, while collecting permanent things for the future—without becoming debt-ridden in the process. Good luck and happy decorating and homemaking.

ONE

WHERE WILL YOU LIVE?

❑

BEFORE you can begin your decorating, you have to have a place to decorate. Finding the right place is an important, sometimes grueling, step towards having an attractive home, one in which you will be happy.

House hunting can be frustrating for anybody, but to the new couple looking for a first home it can be a major dilemma. So I think a discussion of the various living accommodations and considerations in choosing them might be helpful at the start.

The Furnished Apartment

A furnished apartment has much to recommend it as a first home, if, like most young couples, you are not ready for major decorating at the start. The advantages will become increasingly obvious as you read the subsequent chapters on decorating and choosing of furniture, which are based on the plan of collecting good furniture, with a great deal of consideration, *gradually*.

Obviously then, assuming you have practically no furniture in the beginning, you are put into a rather awkward position if you move into an unfurnished place and *have* to acquire some furniture immediately. Urgency and haste, I feel, should never be a part of furniture buying. Thus, unless you have been engaged for a long period of time, during which you have decided what furnishings you want and have collected some of these items—or at least the cash for them—it is a good idea to live in a furnished apartment for the first six months to a year. You can then use this time to assemble sensibly enough things to move into an unfurnished apartment relatively comfortably at the end of this period. Most furnished apartments are sparsely enough furnished to make gradual acquisitions very welcome there, too. It would be well, though, to have access to a basement or similar storage facility for the overflow. Also, when hunting for this furnished apartment, ask about the possibility of a place to work on any furniture you may want to refinish. We have lived in two apartment buildings which had very accommodating janitors who let us use their workshops and tools.

CHOOSING AN AREA

Now that you've established whether you want a furnished apartment or are ready for an unfurnished one, the next thing to consider is the area you want to live in. Granted, this is broadly decided for you by your husband's job, but within most general localities are several smaller areas from which to choose. If you are going to be situated in a city, do you want to live right in the city (if so, what section) or would you rather live in a suburb or way out in the country? (We seem to prefer one extreme or the other, finding suburbs "neither nor," but this is purely personal.) If you've drawn a fair size town as your first home, which section would be best for you?

With these general questions in mind, here are some specific things to be considered.

Commuting distance to your husband's and, if you are working, your job. The commuting cost essentially adds its equivalent to your rent. Also, three hours' commuting is a pretty high price to pay for even the most "perfect" apartment. I know. My husband did it for two years, and it is not worth it.

Congenial neighbors, I think, are one of the most important factors in choosing your apartment. The most charming apartment in the world can be pretty bleak if you have no one to enjoy it with you. When I say neighbors, I do not necessarily mean your immediate neighbors, but those close enough to be seen fairly often. For this reason, charming as that old carriage house may be, if it's in the center of a very wealthy section of middle-aged people and several miles from the closest person who could be called your contemporary, it's questionable if you would be very happy there. The same would apply to moving into a very poor area. Unless of course you *are* either very rich or *really* poor.

How do you know if there *are* congenial people? If you know nothing about the city or town to which you are moving, the best way we have found is to drive around and "case the joint." Stop in neighborhoods that look promising, and glance in grocery stores and notice the people on the streets. If you have found a place you like and want to know who your immediate neighbors are, ask the landlord. He will be glad to give you a run-down on Mrs. Jones who "has three children and another on the way" and lives next door, or "Bob and Mary Smith—a nice young couple who live two doors down and are both going to school."

If a landlord isn't much help, another rather devious way we have found is to ring a few doorbells in the building or neighborhood, on one pretense or another, and find out for ourselves.

General atmosphere will be dictated, to some degree, by what you can afford. But it also goes hand in hand with congenial neighbors, since it is logical that the atmosphere which appeals to you will usually be the one that draws the people with whom you will have most in common. But you should bear in mind the following:

Do you want a quiet, restful atmosphere or do you want one which bustles with activity? A family-type neighborhood, full of young mothers whose primary interest is their precocious offspring, sometimes is a bit tame for the young couple without children who want companionship for all sorts of projects and "high-jinks." Conversely, a neighborhood made up primarily of the latter type can be pretty frustrating to the couple plagued with needing their sleep and baby sitters for their progeny.

Does the sleekness of a new area appeal to you, or would you prefer an older, more settled neighborhood or a really old rundown one which is being pulled up by its bootstraps by enterprising young couples with more ingenuity than money? Do I give myself away as to the one I prefer?

The Apartment Search

You've hit on an area where you "simply must live," now you get down to the actual apartment hunting.

Before you begin you must decide how much you can spend on total rent. This figure should be an all-inclusive one covering everything. How it is used will depend on the sort of apartment you get. Sometimes there will be extras not figured in the rent, such as money necessary for fixing up a place, garage, utilities, etc. (I'll talk about these later). Even though the landlord does not figure these in the rent, you must consider them as part of your total rent.

What size apartment is another thing to decide before starting your quest. Depending on your activities, (Are you both working? Will you have many overnight visitors? Will you entertain a lot?) and the comparative costs in your locality, anything from a one-room efficiency (although these can be pretty trying under any circumstances) to a five-room apartment, with two bedrooms and a dining room, may be the most practical for you. Under average circumstances, with an average amount of entertaining, the best size for a first, unfurnished apartment will probably be what is known as a three- or three-and-one-half-room apartment. This includes a living-dining room, a bedroom, a kitchen, and a bath. It is this kind of apartment I have mainly in mind in the decorating sections of this book, since our first two unfurnished apartments were in this category.

What sort of apartment will it be?—Now you get to the interesting and really fun part—the apartment itself—figuring out its potentials, its decorating possibilities, etc.

The most obvious place to look for an apartment is in one

of the relatively new apartment buildings. From the stand-point of being with your contemporaries, this, if you can afford it, is probably one of the best places for you. Most of these are clean and modern, if somewhat characterless. Here, your main challenge is to provide the character.

If, however, there are none of these fairly new apartment buildings in your area, or if lack of funds or a sense of adventure makes you want to look for something else, you will probably end up looking at older places; either fairly old apartment buildings, which are usually much smaller than the newer ones, or apartments in old houses.

At first glance many of these old buildings seem bleak and uninviting. However, some of the seemingly most discouraging apartments have the potential to be the most charming.

Your rent funds will undoubtedly be low for this, the first real apartment of your own, and with an older place the way you make the most of these funds and your own ingenuity is to keep your sense of humor and your sense of the whimsical. You will probably find the best bargains in houses built fifty to seventy-five years ago and whimsy is one of the main characteristics of these houses. You may be faced with seemingly bleak, dirty, brick and iron gas fireplaces. These can be charming with a coat of white paint given to the brick and jet black to the iron. There probably will be narrow, high windows—some even may be of stained glass. These can be made very attractive with shutters or shades, which I will talk about in the chapter on specific suggestions. The wood-work probably will be dark and uninviting. A coat of light paint to the woodwork as well as to the walls—which invariably also are of too dark a hue for the comparatively dark rooms, will make for a real transformation. The ceilings may look fantastically high—a coat of darker paint will bring them "down" amazingly.

These, then, a few of the most typical "drawbacks" of older houses, can be turned into their most charming features with relative ease. When you go into an "old" house that seems pretty bleak to you, mentally list the things that bother you most and then try to think what you can do to these things (by admitting they are there and playing them up, as with the gas fireplace, or with camouflage, as with the darker ceilings). Be honest with yourself, and think, "Won't these be the very things that will give this room character?"

One important thing to look for is the closet and shelf space. This is necessary, and lack of it is quite a problem. Scanty closet space can be alleviated somewhat with wardrobes and a Victorian coat rack in the hall, however.

If the apartment appeals to your decorating sense and if there is or can be made adequate closet space and if it fits all the other qualifications—grab it before someone else does!

How much will it cost to fix up an older apartment?—Time and ingenuity are the main ingredients for fixing up an older place. Obviously the amount of money you spend should be kept to a minimum. The actual amount of money you can justifiably spend is a simple matter of arithmetic, based on how much you have, how long you will be staying in the apartment, and how much your rent is against what it would be in a comparable place already "fixed up."

In many places the landlord will assume some of these expenses. A landlord likes to see his place "fixed up," and most landlords will cooperate very well. Standard repairs such as those to furnace, plumbing, appliances, if these are his, are his responsibility.

How much "fixing up" he will subsidize will vary greatly from one landlord to the next. Discuss these things with him *before* signing the lease. If the paint is actually in bad condition, he will almost certainly either have the painting done for you (if he does this your color choice will probably be limited) or buy the paint for you. The latter way you usually get your choice of colors and a better job. The landlord, naturally, is delighted he doesn't have to pay someone to do it and will be very agreeable about buying the paint and equipment you want. If, however, the paint is in good condition and you want to change the color, the landlord probably will not be so accommodating and you will have to finance this yourself.

THINGS YOU SHOULD KNOW BEFORE SIGNING A LEASE

Even after finding the most perfect apartment and one that fits all your specifications, there are points to consider before clinching the deal.

Appliances.—Are a stove and refrigerator provided? They probably will be in most towns and cities, particularly if you are renting in an apartment building. But if you are considering a little house, half a double house, or even an apartment in an apartment building in some cities, this equipment may not be provided. Then comes the question, "Is it worth it to buy our own?" New appliances, probably not; used appliances, very possibly. If you find just *"the"* place to live, but it is without appliances and the rent allows the approximately one-hundred-dollar outlay you will have to make for used appliances, they may very well be the answer. I talk about these further under kitchens, in Chapter Ten.

Laundry facilities.—Many apartment buildings provide these in their basements, but if they do not, you will want to know if there is a laundromat close by and if there is not (and even possibly if there is—hauling laundry around gets to be an awful chore and quite expensive), you may have to consider buying your own washing machine. Again the same standards apply to washing machines as to stoves and refrigerators. Although new ones are not usually a good idea—used ones may be. I talk more about these in Chapter Ten also.

Shopping.—You should find out where the closest stores are before renting a place. It can be quite a problem if there aren't grocery stores, or at least delicatessens, in the vicinity.

Transportation.—Are there good public transportation facilities close by? This is quite important, particularly if you live in a city. It is often much more convenient to use these than to drive your own car which creates parking problems, etc.

Trash Removal.—Are cans and removal provided?

Parking.—Is there a garage, and if not, is overnight parking allowed on the street? And is it available?

Pets.—"Will a landlord allow pets?" has always been a

major consideration of ours, as we wouldn't part with our dogs for anything. Usually a lease will say No Pets, but this is often just there to protect the landlord in case your pet misbehaves. (The landlord can then point to the clause and (a) either you get rid of your pet, or (b) he gets rid of you.) So inquire about this if you are interested in housing dogs, cats, birds, white mice, etc.

You probably will not find an apartment which fits all your dreams—you may have to compromise a bit. Decide the factors that are most important to you; hold out for these and hope you get the rest.

TWO

THE PITFALLS OF
BEGINNING DECORATING AND
HOW TO AVOID THEM

◻

THERE is no homemaking endeavor where you are so literally forced to live with your mistakes as in decorating. But with a bit of thought and planning, serious blunders are really rather easy to avoid. First you should be aware of the pitfalls, so let me expound on what I've found to be the common mistakes of beginning decorating and furniture collecting.

The Pitfalls

FURNISHING ALL AT ONCE AND THE BUY-NOW-PAY-LATER PLAN

Let me tell you about a friend of mine whom I'll call Nancy. Shortly after she and her husband, Jim, were married, they were able to buy a little house.

"Now," said Nancy, "we must furnish this house, and," she continued, "a brand-new house needs brand-new furniture."

There was to be a housewarming for the new house, so Nancy felt that complete furnishing was of the utmost urgency. Since all of Nancy and Jim's money was tied up in the house, going to a furniture store with long-term credit was the solution. This they did, gaily buying living room, dining room, kitchen, and bedroom suites, all within one week from one store.

The suites arrived, and the house looked like the furniture store divided into rooms.

It is now five years later—Nancy and Jim are still paying for the furniture; their house still looks like a furniture store, but a shabby and outdated one. With time and three children, the furniture, which was poorly constructed and faddish to begin with, has chipped and deteriorated badly and the faddish design looks heavy and stodgy.

Poor Nancy dislikes it all thoroughly by now, but there is absolutely nothing she can do about it. It is not worth extensive repairs, and since she and Jim are still paying for this furniture they can't start replacing things.

I have another friend, I'll call her Jane and her husband Joe.

Jane and Joe were given a sizeable amount of money as a wedding present, so they decided to buy all their furniture with it.

"Why wait?" they said. "We have the money; we need furniture, so let's buy it all now."

They chose their apartment, which had a living room, dining room, kitchen, and bedroom, and then started to buy their furniture. They were not limited by needing credit as they had a great deal of money. So they marched in and out of all the stores in town and by the end of a week they had accomplished two things; they had spent most of their money—they liked "good things," and had completely furnished their apartment with cherry Early American reproductions.

"So what?" they said to anxious parents who doubted the wisdom of spending all their money at once, "We're going to live with this for the rest of our lives, so we wanted to get the 'best' and, since we had the money, why shouldn't we get it now so we can enjoy it from the beginning?"

It is now four years later. Jane and Joe have been reading "home magazines"; they have gone to a few "home shows"; they have visited the houses of friends; and they have decided that what they *really* like is the atmosphere of Scandinavian contemporary furniture, which is going to be rather difficult to capture with suite upon suite of definitely Early American furniture. "Oh, if we had only waited," moans Jane.

Of the two couples, Nancy and Jim are in the worst position because they are still literally paying for their mistakes and incidentally paying quite dearly, since the rate of interest on a deal such as theirs is outrageously high. Also, since committing themselves to these furniture payments other situations have arisen which make these payments extremely difficult.

Going into heavy debt to buy furniture is always bad business. First, the interest is high; second, you limit yourself as to where you can buy; and third, a young couple's budget is usually low and the future rather uncertain. If you tie up any little surplus you have in long-term obligations, you are in a very bad situation if anything unforeseen arises.

Both the couples were trapped by another decorating pitfall: buying in a hurry—buying all at once.

It is a great temptation, if, as Jane and Joe had, you have the money and a bare place, to want to furnish it immediately, particularly if you think you know just what you want.

But in the beginning when you have just really become interested in furniture (face it, before you were married, even though you were vaguely interested in decorating, you were concentrating much more on the acquisition of a husband and all the things that go with this acquisition—dating, parties, etc.), your tastes are not formulated enough to furnish a place completely. You may not lose your love for Early American furniture, but in becoming familiar with other styles, fabrics, and woods, through friends, magazines, books, and shows, you become aware of their advantages and beauty and may want to incorporate them into your decorating scheme, either completely or mixed with the Early American.

Supposing you *have* studied furniture styles extensively and *know* that you will be happy with an Early American living room from now on: will you be happy with matched reproductions bought en masse from a furniture store? Wouldn't it be more fun to prowl around and ferret out treasures—

antiques as well as reproductions—one by one? This way your room will develop an individuality and character all its own and you will take real pride in each piece.

If, like Jane and Nancy, you buy everything at once, you will probably be pretty frustrated later.

BUYING INEXPENSIVE MAKESHIFTS

When you buy cheap furniture to "make do" for now, not only are you wasting valuable time in working toward any decorating goal, but you take little pride in such purchases. In other words, you have paid out good money for things that are little more than a place to sit or whatever the function happens to be. You won't be really satisfied with your decor until these things are replaced, and, if they are replaced, the money invested in them can be considered literally wasted.

On the other hand, as new expenses appear, in the form of additional schooling, an automobile, children, etc., you may very well put off replacing these things indefinitely, thereby continuing to live in a hodgepodge of makeshifts. This seems such a shame when it is so unnecessary.

LETTING FADS DICTATE YOUR DECOR

All too often I've seen my associates be caught in the fad trap.

It is very easy to be swayed by the fashion of the moment, but don't. Nothing can look as outdated as last year's craze. Its demise is only natural because even if it was a good idea at the start, it loses its charm as more and more ill-thought-out and gimmicky versions appear. By the time the fad is replaced by a new one, everyone is thoroughly sick of it.

Your decor should express your personality, not the fashions of the time. However, if the two should coincide, that is, if independent of the rage, you are enamored with Biedermeier furniture, don't panic; use it in a careful and individual way and your decor will survive. After all Biedermeier furnishings have been around for over a hundred years.

BEING STOPPED BY NOT KNOWING WHERE TO START

Finally, there is the person who basically has all the qualifications for good decorating; good taste, an awareness of the virtues of many different furniture styles, and a real flair, but feels frustrated by a meager furniture allowance. She doesn't quite know where to start with it, and is afraid of making a mistake. So she does nothing.

I have another friend who did just this. For two years she and her husband lived in a bare, bleak apartment, without even unpacking all their boxes, because, poor girl, she just "didn't know where to start."

Now, before I discourage you right into the last trap, let's turn to the positive side.

Avoiding the Pitfalls

If, as in so many contests today, I were asked to write in twenty-five words or less my basic philosophy of decorating, it would read something like this: *Collect gradually things that will be a permanent part of your home while acknowledging the fact that your tastes will change.* I would, though, feel a certain frustration at not being able to elaborate on this basic premise, so that is just what I'm going to do.

REALIZE THAT YOUR TASTES WILL CHANGE

When I mentioned, at the beginning of the chapter, that your tastes will change, I was probably hooted at with varying degrees of scorn. But I feel strongly about this. True, some people's tastes will change much more than others. At one extreme is the individual whose taste does not actually change, just broadens, and at the other is the person who does a complete switch.

When I first became aware of furniture, I could see nothing but Early American antiques. You will probably gather as you read this book that these are still among my favorites. But my narrow-mindedness was challenged rather drastically one day when I first considered taking up Interior Decorating as a career.

I was talking to a friend who was an Interior Designer, and was saying that I thought I might have trouble since there were certain periods which I particularly disliked.

"Why?" she challenged. I didn't have any real reason other than I just did not like them.

Then the friend told me that when she first became conscious of furniture, indeed even when she first started her career, she too felt just this way. But as she was forced through clients' preferences to study thoroughly the styles which she had not liked, she realized that every period, every style, in its pure sense, does have its beauty and its charm. "It is up to anyone interested in decorating to look for these attributes," she finished.

With this in mind I began to examine the periods I'd heretofore deliberately ignored and found this indeed to be true. I still think that the blatant, clumsy lines of some Victorian furniture, for example, are grotesque. But there are pieces of it that are delicate and graceful and still others that are whimsical and appealing to use in ingenious ways. Most "Grand Rapids Modern" is angular and sterile, but the Scandinavians, in particular, have captured a lovely fluid grace in much of their contemporary furniture that cannot be excelled.

I have also found that much of the Moorish furniture, which I'd thought to be heavy and ponderous, has real character. The same applies to Jacobean furniture, and I have decided to incorporate some of these into my decorating.

Where before I wanted to be a purist—have everything authentically Early American—now I want to blend some of these styles. This, you may be thinking, will make for a real hodgepodge, but, if done carefully, observing a few basic principles, it can be done very satisfactorily. I will go into this, in detail, in a later chapter.

"All right," you say, "so my tastes will change. Isn't it risky to buy anything then?" The answer is, it doesn't have to be, and the explanation of this brings me to the next rule of decorating.

Use simplicity and ingenuity and *consider everything as a permanent investment.* Ask yourself, "How will I use it now, and how will I use it later?"

Probably two of the first things you will need are a couch and a chair for your living room. Now these are two of the most expensive and important pieces of your decor so it is rather contradictory to all I've been saying to rush out and buy them, as such, right in the beginning. So ask yourself, "What can I buy that will serve this purpose now and a foreseeable purpose in the future and will be of quality and simplicity and within my budget?"

For example, I solved the couch problem with a basic studio couch of good design and a neutral color. (This, too, is important for your large pieces at this time—accent pieces and slip covers can sport the bright colors. I'll talk more about this later.) A studio couch serves as a couch and bed for guests in the beginning and will do beautifully in a sitting room, study, or game room later.

For the chair, I settled on a Yugoslavian basket chair for $11.00 at a roadside basket stand. It is still a handsome part of our living room, but when I feel I can part with it there, it will be attractive in a study, game room, or even on a porch. Both pieces of furniture are simple, versatile, and well-made, insuring durability and a quality of blending with any period or style I choose to put with them.

This thinking can be applied to any beginning purchase you make. In effect, what you are doing is achieving two things, getting the things you need to live comfortably in the beginning and acquiring permanent items for your home, yet not limiting yourself.

Buy the best of what you are buying. Don't compromise by buying an inexpensive version of a more elaborate item. This is false economy; you will not be truly satisfied with it—nor will it stand the test of time. Instead, buy a real quality piece of a less ambitious nature. This is not to say that once you have determined what is a quality piece that you should not shop around for a good buy on it. Check discount stores, furniture showrooms, etc., for the best price.

BE DARING IN YOUR IDEAS

Up to now the tone of this chapter has been a cautious one but as caution is part of good decorating, so too is daring. Sound contradictory? It isn't! While careful planning and buying can't be stressed often enough, this prudence shouldn't permeate your decorating *ideas*. They should be gay, alive, individual—even daring.

Sticking to "safe" conventional ideas can make for a rather uninspired room. It may be perfectly acceptable—in perfectly good taste, but it probably won't be particularly distinctive.

As you study furniture styles and decorating ideas in the ways I suggest, you may get some fairly unconventional ideas for your decor. You may be inclined to reject them as being too "different." But don't; consider the ideas a bit more. Think how they fit your way of life and the atmosphere you want to live in. If they seem right for you, take the plunge and dare to be different. Don't be afraid of the unusual. It's what will take your decor out of the commonplace and make it special.

THREE

THE WONDERS OF COLOR

COLOR, I feel, is the single most important ingredient in decorating.

Color has the ability to create a mood. What is your reaction as you go into a room of stark blacks and whites with an unexpected, sudden splash of red? It can make you fairly tingle with excitement and a sense of the dramatic. In the same way a room of limpid blues and greens can give you a sense of tranquility and refreshment and a room of warm mustards, oranges, browns, and greens can make you feel warm and cozy.

Color can suggest a country or a style. Try to picture any wood piece you own lacquered black and trimmed with gold. Wouldn't there be a hint of the Orient? And who can see soft pinks and roses mixed with pale opalescent aquas and not think of the Romantic periods of the French kings.

Color has optical illusion properties; it can, figuratively, enlarge or diminish a room or a piece of furniture according to your needs. If you have ever seen a seemingly cramped, dark little room suddenly transformed into a comfortable "spacious" room with a coat of white or other light paint, you are well aware of the "magic" of color. Later in the chapter I discuss in detail how you can achieve specific effects with color.

Now, when you are moving about, is the time for you to experiment with color. See which "moods," which colors, you can live with season in and season out. Some color schemes you will find just right for one season but too "hot" for another. Now, while your housing is temporary, while you are painting relatively small areas in apartments and other "temporary" living quarters and are using the inexpensive slip-cover and curtain materials, which I so heartily recommend, is the time to find out about color and what it can do for you. Do, however, keep the permanent pieces, which you are gradually acquiring, in a neutral or color you *know* you like.

Colors can be the main charm of an inexpensive room. So try out any wild colors you have a hankering for at this point and let them add gaiety and personality to your modest quarters. This experimenting is fun and is preparing you and formulating your tastes, so when the time comes for you to make big investments in "permanent" colors such as upholstery, paint for your house, etc., you can do it with conviction and no regrets.

How Much Color?

First, you must think of *your apartment as a whole*. When considering it in its entirety, there are three ways you can use color.

First, you can have one basic color scheme throughout. This way you have the effect of one room flowing into another. This can be effective in some homes, but it also can be monotonous, and in the case of a new "decorator" doesn't give much chance for experimenting.

The second way is a blending of one room into another. This method is rather like making a braided rug. You start with three colors. Then, you continue with two of the original colors but drop the third and pick up a new one instead. Work these three, then drop another of the original colors and pick up still another color and so on. Thus, there is a fluid transition of colors. This is particularly effective when one room leads into another, but you don't want to use exactly the same colors, as in a living room with a dining area.

The third way is to consider each room a *separate challenge*. In using color this way, you do not think of one room in relation to another, but complete in itself. This thinking lets you pick a separate color scheme for each room. This method is particularly fun for the new decorator and gives her a wide range of experience. However, it would not be good for rooms that very definitely flow into one another, such as a living room and a dining area.

Color Within a Room

As there are several ways to consider color in relation to your entire apartment, so are there several different basic ways to use color within a room.

"How many colors may be used in one room?" is one of the questions you have asked, I am sure. The answer seems to change with the trends. One year the home magazines are pushing the monochromatic color schemes. The next year they will be saying firmly "two main colors and one accent color." And still another year they will say "use as many colors as you like as long as they are harmonious." Since all of these concepts have been in vogue at one time or another, it is safe to assume that any of them is "correct" and can be used to advantage. It is up to you.

Nature seems to be the best craftsman of all with colors. So let's let her help us define the different possibilities.

MONOCHROMATIC COLOR SCHEME

This, as the name implies, is the use of varying shades and intensities of *one* color.

Picture a moonlit night with its various gradations of silvers, silvery grays, darker grays, and blacks and you have a lovely version of a monochromatic color scheme.

Interesting shapes, a variance in textures, beautiful woods and designs and interesting accessories are shown off to good advantage with this treatment, and, indeed, as in nature, are the very things which foil monotony.

TWO MAIN COLORS AND ONE ACCENT COLOR

This is probably the easiest and surest way to get a good and fairly versatile effect.

Again, nature has produced such effects everywhere you look. Blue and green water lapping against golden sand, and freshly plowed rich brown earth against yellow wheat fringed with green trees, are more examples from the master decorator of all—nature.

A hint here—follow nature's example. Keep colors rich, but subtle. "Straight from the paint box" colors are usually stark and harsh. Also, as does nature, keep your color tones and variances in good balance.

A MULTITUDE OF HARMONIOUS COLORS

"Horrors, what a mess," you may be saying.

But haven't you ever been delighted by a multicolor bed of tulips or, to cite man's creations, been enthralled with the rich and endless colors of a kaleidoscope or a stained-glass window?

Here, again, you should have a good plan before you start so your colors will be in good blending tones, well-balanced, and interrelating harmoniously with one another. Fabrics should be kept fairly uniform and other design and detail should be kept simple and uncluttered, so the result will not be confusion.

In Summary

There are no hard and fast rules about using color. Who would have thought of using orange and fuchsia together some years ago, but today this "clashing" color combination is thought to be ultrasophisticated and chic. So, the best plan, rather than being governed by a lot of "color rules" and fads which may be outdated tomorrow, is to go out and notice colors: look at colors in nature; look at colors in paintings, magazines, shop windows, and clothes; collect paint chips from your paint dealer and juggle them to find combinations which please you. Soon you will get a feel for color which will yield much more satisfying results and will make for far more originality than being a slave to the current trends.

Specific Effects

As I said in the beginning of this chapter, there are many things color can do for you. These things will become increasingly obvious as you acquire your "feel" for color, but to get you started I would like to give you a few basic ideas.

MOODS THROUGH COLOR

The following is a list of atmospheres a room can create, and the colors that help to accomplish it. Of course, there is a great overlapping. For example, the "coolest" room may be made "warm" by a splash or two of a bright color or vice versa, and the intensity and shading of a color can change its atmosphere. Also, there are other factors which contribute to a room's overall effect, but, these being in accord, here are the colors and their adjectives.

Warm, mellow, and comfortable:	The earth tones, fall colors, browns, beiges, oranges, mustards, and dull greens.
Cool, tranquil, and restful:	Blues, greens, off-whites, lemon yellows, and grays.
Cozy, charming, gay:	Clear vivid colors, red, white, blue, green.
Striking:	Black, white and red, touches of gold.
Sophisticated:	Muted colors, beiges, grays, and off-white.
Formal:	Soft colors, roses, blues, beiges, off-white. Or, conversely, some rich, full-bodied colors, such as wine, royal blue.

PERIODS THROUGH COLOR

Each period and style also has colors which exemplify it. These colors stick pretty well to the above list; if the period was formal, the colors used were the very same colors we consider today as contributing to formality. These colors created the atmosphere then just as they do now. So, if you want to impart a Victorian atmosphere, and also formality, you may, as the two are compatible—indeed, almost synonomous.

If you want a contemporary look, then the clean, cool colors of its restful design are in order. Since it is also essentially a gay style, these same colors should be vivid and crisp.

The ways colors were used did, however, vary in different periods. For instance, many of the Early American houses show a darker woodwork than wall color, the woodwork being either a darker value of the wall color or a different color altogether. The French showed off their lovely pastels in stripes, refined prints, and damasks, and so on.

Once you get a feel for color and design, decorating is like a marvelously satisfying crossword puzzle, with the different aspects reacting to and interrelating logically with one another. The end effect is a logical relation of all the different facets.

OPTICAL ILLUSIONS THROUGH COLOR

Another thing to consider when choosing your colors, particularly the colors for walls and ceiling, is the optical illusion you would like to create. Dark colors tend to make a room or object look smaller while light colors have the opposite effect. Therefore, a coat of light paint can actually "enlarge" a dark little room. As a dark color pulls in a room, it can also be made to do the same thing with a single wall, the end wall of a long narrow room, perhaps, or if your high ceilings bother you, they can be "lowered" by a coat of paint of a darker tone than the walls.

Another optical illusion with color is made with contrasts. A contrasting color makes a wall or an article stand out, makes it a focal point, while colors close in value give a serene blending effect, and no one object is made prominent. Either method may be used effectively, depending on a room's good or bad features and the overall effect you wish to achieve.

LIGHT THROUGH COLOR

Most people want their rooms to be light and airy in the daytime. You can make the most of the natural light in your apartment by using the proper wall color. If a room tends to be too dark, white or a pale color will lighten it considerably. If it's too bright, a dull tone will cut down the glare.

Basic Color Plans

Once you are aware of color and know what effect you wish to create and what colors you want to use, you may still have questions: "Where do I start?" "How do I use colors?"

There are several ways you can use your color schemes. Many of these ways will depend on the optical illusions mentioned above and some will depend on your personal preference, but in any case you should have an overall plan before you begin.

LET THE BACKGROUND SET THE SCHEME

Have your background, that is your rugs, curtains, and walls, an overall blending of one of your colors and then use that background color intensified, along with your other colors in a well-balanced fashion around the room.

For example, a mustard, green, and orange color scheme could have as its blending color a pale mustard. The walls, curtains, and floors would be of this hue. A piece of furniture would bring in a darker mustard, as a connection with its background and then this whole mustard blending could be punctuated with oranges and greens. This method is good when you want a fairly uniform tranquil effect, and where you deliberately do not want the emphasis on the windows and floors. This treatment is, of course, ideal for a monochromatic color scheme.

LET A PATTERN SET THE SCHEME

Have part of your background a neutral (your rug and walls maybe) such as an off-white, or a pale-gray or beige. Let the curtains be of a pattern, stripe or plaid, boasting the colors which will be picked up in the furniture. Again, these colors should be used in a well-balanced manner around the room. For example, off-white walls and rugs could be the background for bold green and blue plaid curtains from which the furniture takes its cue and emerges in the same shades of blue and green. This, of course, puts stress on the windows, which can be good or bad, depending on the size and position of the windows and the curtains used.

The effect achieved by this treatment is usually more striking and dramatic than the first method and can be used to advantage when a contemporary look is wanted. I have found it to be easy and effective. Taking colors from a patterned fabric give your colors a purpose, a reason for being, and the effect is usually harmonious.

This treatment has many modifications and can be used well in a variation of the preceding plan also. For instance, in the mustard room I spoke of, the curtains could have a mustard background with a pattern incorporating the other room colors.

A room's color key could also be a slipcover for a couch or other large piece of furniture. Or you might let a patterned rug set the color scheme for your room. The background could be the same color as your wall while the design would have the colors of your furnishings. A braided or oriental rug could also set the color scheme.

In any case, if you use a pattern in a room, either in curtains, slipcovers, or as a floor cover, let it hold the colors which will then reappear in the room. Often a pattern fabric, having the colors you want, is a good thing with which to start. You can then, with a swatch of this material clutched tightly in your hand, go around matching fabrics and paints to it.

A final word of advice in choosing your colors; use colors

which will set off your prized possessions. If you are putting an emphasis on lovely mellow woods, you will want colors that bring out their richness. If you are collecting copper and brass, the same colors will emphasize these. On the other hand, if silver is your passion, you will want colors which make the most of its elegant coolness.

Color is your best friend and ally in decorating on a budget. You have experimented no doubt with "make-up." You know how it can be used to tone down bad features and emphasize good ones—so it is in decorating. An ugly, grotesque piece of furniture dragged from someone's basement can at least be made gay and whimsical with a bright coat of paint to blend with your color scheme and in turn with your decorating scheme.

A bad feature of a room can be almost hidden with a color which will blend unobtrusively with a good feature. Good features of a room can in turn be emphasized by a contrasting color which proudly heralds them to the eye. Color is a tonic. Color is a tranquilizer. Become familiar with it and many of your problems will be over.

FOUR

KNOWING AND USING
PERIOD FURNITURE

◻

ONE of the facets of decorating I've been mentioning and will continue to mention is period furnishings. Period furnishings can be described as objects attributed to a specific period in history with distinctive characteristics which identify them as such.

In order to choose your furniture wisely and to decorate satisfactorily with a little budget as well as a large one, you should know something about the basic periods and styles and how they can be made to work for you. The more you find out about the different styles and periods the easier it will be for you to formulate your lasting tastes and wants in furniture. As I've said in a previous chapter, each period has something to offer, so look into them all before drawing any firm conclusions as to your likes and dislikes. You owe this to yourself, because it would be too bad to concentrate entirely on Scandinavian contemporary "because that's what I've always liked" and find out five years later, entirely by accident, that Louis XV is delightful.

In this chapter I give you the basic ways to use any period's furniture and accessories, and a brief breakdown of the different periods. At the end of the book there is an outline of the significant periods and their most obvious identifying features for easy reference. But these will not give you the flavor, the atmosphere, of the different periods and countries; this you must discover for yourself.

26

PERIOD DECORATING NEEDN'T BE EXPENSIVE

"Period furnishing on a little budget?" you may be scoffing.

Just because you're on a little budget is no reason why you can't be working toward almost any period's atmosphere you like. I'm talking about *elegant* decorating, not just decorating, and the ingredient which replaces money is knowledge!! If you know what gives a particular period style its atmosphere, its charm, and what its key features are, you can work toward achieving this charm by the use of colors typical of the style, accessories with the same flavor as the style, and furniture which suggests one style while actually being another, less expensive one.

For instance, suppose you have a hankering for an early Spanish room: Now original Moorish furniture is quite expensive but you could get the effect through color—primarily blues and reds against stark white walls, regal horizontal lines, and the use of certain Victorian iron accessories in place of the old Spanish ones.

If you choose a period style whose original furniture is accessible at reasonable prices, fine, you can collect the authentic pieces too. In Chapter Five I discuss how some of these pieces can be your very best buys.

BECOME FAMILIAR WITH DIFFERENT PERIODS

The only way to become really aware of the atmosphere of a period is rather obvious—see it—not just as a piece or two but as a whole room or setting, capturing the feeling of the time. There are several ways to do this; one is to go to museums—large ones, such as the Metropolitan Museum of Art in New York—which have rooms, with various pieces of furniture and accessories from different periods and nationalities, or to actual old houses, castles, etc., which, left almost intact, have been opened to the public. Also, to learn about early American places, visit restorations such as Sturbridge Village, Massachusetts, Williamsburg, Virginia, and the Henry Ford Museum and Greenfield Village, in Dearborn, Michigan, which although touristy, have spent millions of dollars to do just what we're talking about—capture to the last detail the atmosphere of a period.

As you might suppose, in America it is much easier to find examples of authentic American periods than those of other nationalities; however, there are places—museums and private endeavors—which have looked to other countries. Many museums have authentic European rooms which have been acquired by bringing the rooms, in sections (paneling, beams, ceilings, windows, furnishings, etc.) from abroad and then rebuilding them into the museum. The University of Pittsburgh has a remarkable collection of foreign period atmosphere in its International classrooms. These, opening off a hall encircling the Cathedral of Learning, capture the flavor of eighteen different countries, through the painstaking effort of top foreign designers and decorators.

The easiest way to study periods is with illustrated books. There are hundreds of books dealing with different periods. These can be history books, architectural books, travel books, or actual furniture books.

One which depicts very well this country's early atmosphere and one of which I'm very fond is a book called *A Second Treasury of Early American Houses* by Dorothy and Richard Pratt. This book shows, with magnificent illustrations, many, many houses from different sections of the country, all retaining their original, or similar to original, furniture and embellishments. The exteriors, as well as the interiors, are shown, and as you look at one of the interiors, with its authentic wall and floor treatment, its lovely old furniture, and its warm, spacious air, you begin to *feel* Americana.

Turning to Europe, what could be a better guide to the charm of Louis XIV, Louis XV, and Louis XVI, than an illustrated book on Versailles. Many of these books may be found in your local library.

The third way to familiarize yourself with the different periods is to go to shows, exhibits, and individuals' houses where a particular atmosphere is being stressed. This is not the best way, because you usually are not getting the pure period from which to draw your own conclusions, but instead are getting someone else's interpretation of a period. This can be bad and often not do justice to a period at all; on the other hand, it can be good. It depends on who has "done" the exhibit or room, what he is trying to achieve, and his knowledge of what he is doing. Look into these factors before drawing any conclusions about a style or period from such an exhibit.

If you follow some, or, if possible, all of the above suggestions as well as study a bit about the various styles, you should be able to decide which periods—styles—have the characteristics and the atmosphere that you would most like to live with.

SIGNIFICANT AMERICAN AND EUROPEAN STYLES

Since it is rather difficult to remember, particularly in the beginning, which periods fit in where, I'm inserting an appendix showing the chronological order of the primary American and major European periods and styles, and their most obvious and usual identifying characteristics. As you can see, the description of each period is sketchy and brief at best, so you will want to read books on antiques which study the different periods and their characteristics in detail. The outlines are designed as a ready reference and an organizational aid to get you started. A lot of these examples you will not be dealing with *per se* in the beginning, or maybe not at all, but it is well to familiarize yourself with them and their atmosphere since you might want to work around or toward any one of them.

These outlines deal primarily with the formal styles of the period. Unfortunately (since it is mainly the country pieces which are accessible to us in the beginning) it is almost impossible to deal with all the country-cottage trends since they were mainly regional adaptations of the formal styles. In general, they ran a bit behind and spanned a much longer period of time than their formal origin.

CONTEMPORARY FURNITURE

So far I've been discussing traditional furniture. So that you, with a leaning toward contemporary, won't feel neglected, let me say that I think traditional styles merit the longest discussion, because it is from traditional furniture that modern furniture has evolved. I feel that whether you are ultimately going to use traditional or contemporary furniture (in the broadest sense, your two choices) an awareness of the traditional is necessary for perspective and choice. Much contemporary furniture is actually a modern interpretation of a traditional and/or foreign style—one of the most handsome chairs to come out of Sweden recently is, in essence, a Windsor chair.

Presently there are three main contemporary "looks."

Scandinavian.—This, as I've indicated, has drawn often from the simple lines of the early relatively primitive styles of America, England, and Europe. These lines have been combined with lovely mellow woods and rough-textured homespun-type fabrics also reminiscent of the early handwoven cloth of our ancestors. The result—lovely graceful pieces of furniture which on their own have a warm casualness and blend beautifully with all but the most formal of their forerunners.

Oriental.—The Oriental contemporary is really a "look," in that it is a style which boasts very few pieces which could be called "Oriental contemporary." Stark colors—red and white, black, and gold, in particular, or dull earth tones, low angular furniture, floor cushions, a suggestion of ancient carved Oriental relics, screens, and scrolls are just a few of its characteristics. All these combine to make an atmosphere of an ageless orient while still giving the impression of ultramodern.

American.—Rather than being a style of its own, American contemporary draws from America, Europe, and the Orient, getting both traditional and contemporary ideas from them, sometimes with very good results as in the collections of some of the more expensive American designers and companies.

But often American contemporary furniture emerges as modern for modern's sake—stark, angular, institutional-looking and poorly made. These examples, I feel, are what have made traditionalists justifiably scornful of contemporary furniture.

Good furniture shows, company showrooms (listed in the Yellow Pages of most cities' telephone books), museums stressing modern art and trends and/or the Orient, and books and magazines are the ways to become familiar with the real beauty of contemporary furniture and what it has to offer.

DECORATING WITH PERIOD FURNITURE

The chameleon qualities of good furniture are amazing and offer several different ways to use period furniture. The most obvious way, of course, is to use one period entirely, sticking to the objects and/or reproductions of one period (again, I am considering contemporary as a period, also). The advantages of this way are that if you know your period well, and I hope you do, your chances of making drastic mistakes are slim. These assets, however, are also the pitfalls of this way of decorating. Your room, or rooms, may end up so "perfect" as to look calculated, and in the case of antiques, look like a museum, or with modern, like a decorator's showroom.

A friend of mine has a lovely old house which she and her husband have completely done over themselves and furnished entirely with Early American antiques. Everything is authentic down to the bare floor in the dining room and the straight uncomfortable chairs in the living room. It is charming. It has captured perfectly the charm of Americana. It would do a museum proud, but somehow it lacks the "lived-in" look that makes a house home. It is too perfect.

If you are a purist and, after much consideration and study, this is the way you decide to decorate, by all means do, but beware of this one pitfall. Look for the things of the period that will make your apartment or house cozy and comfortable. Also, vary the woods and textures. You might bring in some wrought iron, brass, marble, or painted surfaces, if these belong to your period, to blend with the natural woods which you'll probably have also. Look, too, for the unusual pieces which don't "scream" your period as well as those things which do. In general, guard against the calculated and the too obvious.

A variation of the pure form of decorating which often eliminates its problems is first to capture the flavor of a period by primarily using things of, or suggestive of, a certain period. Then blend in accessories of other periods or countries for interest. After all, this was done by the mates of the old sailing ships who brought back treasures from as far away as the Orient to decorate their, up to then, conservative homes.

The third, and probably the most challenging and rewarding, way of decorating, is the combination of two or more styles. To understand this way, you must first accept the premise that the good, pure form furniture of one period can be blended satisfactorily with accessories and background of another, provided that their scale and flavor is similar (in general it is best to combine the formal styles with other formal styles and the informal with the informal). Indeed, one can have a "period" while having very few items authentic to that period, since the color, background treatment, and accessories primarily "make" a period. Therefore someone who, as I do, likes the color, the freshness, and the lightheartedness of Scandinavian contemporary, while being very fond of antiques can, "have his cake and eat it, too."

I have seen ornately carved Italian chairs, stripped of their varnish and polished to look like rich sandalwood, beautifully blended into an oriental-flavored room. I've also seen Victorian chests and chairs, antiqued with white and gold paint, made to look very French.

A departure from the blending of periods is the deliberate introduction of contrasts. This is a dramatic treatment used primarily in contemporary rooms to relieve monotony. One or two contrasting pieces such as carved European chests are a bold interest statement and an effective foil to the simple lines of the contemporary pieces.

And then there is our own interplay of Scandinavian and

Early American decor. Our furniture is, for the most part, simple, American, country antiques. Yet our first apartment was described by all who saw it as Scandinavian in flavor. This effect was achieved mainly through color, fabrics, and the similar characteristics of the natural wood of our antiques and that used in the Scandinavian countries today.

We used startling blues and greens against a cream background. Our curtains were a rough-textured blue and green plaid and the couch and chair slip covers picked up the same blues and greens in similar handwoven-type fabrics. This sort of fabric, although very Scandinavian, goes beautifully with antiques, since it is reminiscent of the homespun materials of their time. The color and design make the difference. Since many of our antiques are low and small in scale, we were able to fit in two Danish chairs, which although typically Danish, had as their origin Windsor chairs, and so blended in well and in turn made our real Windsors look Danish. The whole room was a careful combination of two styles, with an occasional item of neither style. Since the colors, designs, and some accessories were Scandinavian, so was the room.

In a subsequent apartment I changed the color scheme to dull mustards, browns, and greens, exchanged the contemporary-looking curtains for an Americana print, put my copper and brass in strategic positions, and presto, the Early American pieces became strikingly what they were— antiques!—and the Danish chairs became less Danish and more Windsor. People now talked about our Early American decor.

I hope these examples have demonstrated two things to you. First, the versatility of basic furniture of good design, and second, that which I'm stressing throughout, the importance of choosing your furniture carefully and not buying your permanent, large, upholstered pieces until you know definitely the atmosphere you want to live with.

The points to keep in mind when incorporating several styles or periods are fairly simple. First choose one period's atmosphere as your guide and let it be your background, and, although not absolutely necessary, have one or two good examples of your period to emphasize it. Stick primarily to simple uncluttered lines; you can use the more ornate as your accent pieces if the period you have chosen is one of the more elaborate ones. Watch the scale. You don't want some pieces drastically overpowering other pieces. The happy result of this technique is the general effect of a period, with the specific trademark of the owner.

FIVE

BUYING ANTIQUES

THOSE of you who are contemporary fans may think that I lean too much toward antiques, and overemphasize them. I stress them because I feel that no matter which periods you particularly like, a knowledge of antiques—their periods, their woods, where to find them, how to buy them and what they can do for you—is a great help in successful decorating. As I've tried to point out, an antique or two can give an added bit of interest to the most contemporary room, and if you insist, many of them can be made to look contemporary themselves.

Here let me qualify the term antique. Technically, an antique is an object made before 1830. This is the date set in 1930 when the United States government ruled that a piece had to be one hundred years old to be considered an antique, and thus admitted duty free to this country. However, the word has fallen into general use, and I use it to describe any period piece up to about 1900. A period piece (as I've said before) is one which has come out of a specific period in history.

Making Antiques a Good Investment

It is a popular misconception of people not familiar with antiques to think of them as being exorbitantly expensive, as witness the reaction of a recent acquaintance of an antique collector friend of mine. The acquaintance who, it turned out, had her house "done" in Early American reproductions, was visiting my friend for the first time. "Your antiques are beautiful," said the girl wistfully, "I couldn't possibly afford them." My friend answered honestly, "I couldn't afford the reproductions." Strange as it may sound, this is quite true.

Good reproductions of many antique pieces are much more expensive than the originals, and at that, usually can't compare in workmanship and lovely woods. Furthermore, purely from an investment standpoint, the value of antiques is always on the rise. So it would be safe to say that if you buy an antique at a good price today, should you want to, you could sell it tomorrow for more than you paid for it—particularly if it is in the rough when you buy it and you restore it. New furniture, however, is nothing more than "used furniture" as soon as you take it out of the store, and as such, worth a fraction of its original value for resale.

Antiques are not *always* a bargain, though. Once you get the bug, antiquing becomes a real fever. Since some of the characteristics of genuine antiques are hard to define, there are individuals who capitalize on the novice's enthusiasm by charging far too much, and even worse, passing off reproductions or partial reproductions (here I am referring to antiques which, much the worse for wear, have been revamped with new materials; for instance, a table—maybe only the top is original while its legs, drawers, etc. have been replaced) as "authentic" pieces. There is nothing wrong with reproductions, mind you, but you should know when you are getting one. So it is well to be aware of certain things before you begin your quest for antiques. Following is a list and discussion of the ways to avoid some of the pitfalls of antiquing.

Know your dealer.—This precaution belongs both at the beginning and at the end of the list since unless you have a thoroughly reliable dealer you should not consider buying until you know the things which follow. But a good dealer, an honest dealer, a dealer genuinely interested in antiques can be a great help to a young couple just becoming acquainted with them.

We were lucky when we first began antiquing to have a friend introduce us to a thoroughly honest, well-informed dealer, who in turn took us under his wing, so to speak, and by talking and showing us things, taught us much of what we now know. In turn, whenever possible, we buy our things from him. If you can find such a dealer, one whom you can be sure is totally honest (and sad as it seems, I'm afraid there aren't too many), or a friend with a real knowledge of antiques, you're truly in luck. Don't be shy; ask as many questions as you can think of, for this is the best way to learn.

If, however, you do not have a reliable introduction to such a person, this category very definitely belongs at the end of the chapter, because there are many things you should know before going into the antique "fray." When you are aware of enough of these things to want some first-hand experiences, you are probably still not ready to buy big pieces, but do go into shops (if possible, find out the shop's reputation first), look around, test your knowledge, and ask questions and prices of the dealer for comparison and familiarization. Then, if you must, treat yourself (and the dealer) to a little bit of brass, copper, or china, which will be decorative, but not a major investment.

As you become familiar with antiques, you will be better qualified to buy more ambitious pieces on your own, and remember, when you don't know your dealer, you *are* on your own. Don't be taken in by any fancy claims. Unless your experience is considerable, or you have complete faith in your dealer, it is well at any time to have any really expensive piece examined by an expert.

Know your woods.—There are certain readily distinguishable characteristics such as color and grain, which once learned, make identification of raw woods fairly easy. I say raw woods, because often antiques as well as new furniture have elaborate finishes and stains which hide the natural attributes of their woods. Any antique which is thus covered up should have several places scraped on it to reveal the natural wood. If there are no such places, you are quite within your rights (indeed, you definitely should) to ask to have several places scraped at strategic points. One scraping is not sufficient as woods may vary throughout a piece; for instance, the top of a table may be one wood, the legs another, and the drawers still another.

If you are still not sure of the wood, a further test is one with oil. Have with you a little jar of boiled linseed oil and a dauber. Apply a thin "skin" of the oil to the scraped areas. This brings out the natural color of the wood and makes identification fairly certain. Many people don't realize that all you need to achieve the color you associate with a particular wood is oil. I'll talk about this further in the refinishing section.

You can get a fairly good idea of the character of the different woods from their description in books and magazines (there is a good pamphlet available for 50¢ from the Superintendent of Documents, U.S. Government Printing Office, Washington 25, D.C., entitled *Wood: Colors and Kinds*. It is *Agricultural Handbook No. 101*) but you should see these woods, both "raw" and daubed with oil, before considering yourself a reliable authority. Go to a lumber yard and get little wood samples (these will give you a good idea of wood grains, but their color will vary slightly from antiques—age gives a mellowness to antique wood which is not to be found in new). Better still, if you have found yourself a helpful antique dealer or knowledgeable friend, get him to give you a short "course in woods," complete with examples. I might mention here that the woods you are most liable to run into in your quest for antiques are: pine, poplar, chestnut, oak, hickory (only in chair spindles), cherry, walnut, and, occasionally in formal pieces, mahogany.

Know your periods.—This, as I've said before, is important to your overall decorating, and something you should know in the very beginning. A general knowledge of periods should be the deciding factor in the kind of furniture you choose. But a knowledge of the fine details of a specific period is necessary for the successful purchase of its antiques.

You should know, besides the characteristics of the period, the construction used at that time; were wooden pegs used, or were square nails in vogue? What kind of joints were used?

Dovetailing, the method used to join the front of a drawer to its sides, tells much about a piece with a drawer. Early pieces have hand dovetailing, employing varying shapes, sizes, and crudeness, while, since the machine age, most dovetailing has been done by machine, with a regular precision which identifies it as such. However, the machine was not so quick to affect the country pieces as those made in the city. Therefore, most country pieces continued to be fashioned with hand dovetails for some time after the beginning of the machine age.

Knowing something of the history of a period's furniture, where it was used and what it was used for, will dictate somewhat the condition the piece should be in. For instance, if you know a hutch table was probably used in a country kitchen, you will know that those dents along the top of yours very likely were made by a cherry pitter, meat grinder or some other early implement which was attached to the table. You should know, too, that a very old piece, particularly a country piece, will have its edges slightly worn and rounded. If it does not, its authenticity is to be doubted.

Also, it is well to know something about the tools used during the different periods as their identifying marks give a reliable idea of the age of a piece. For instance, a buzz-saw (always power driven) was first introduced into the United States in 1825, but it wasn't generally used until sometime later. Thus, if any furniture attributed to any period before American Victorian bears buzz-saw marks (a series of concentric archlike scratches forming a circle 6 to 18 inches in diameter, usually found on the interior parts of pieces) it is not authentic. Earlier pieces may have straight saw marks (a series of straight scratches, either perpendicular or at a slight angle across the face of the wood). Clever cabinet makers can "antique" a piece by marking it, etc., but true signs of age are hard to manufacture. *Field Guide to Early American Furniture*, by Thomas H. Ormsbee, has a chapter entitled "Detecting Genuine Pieces," which is very worthwhile reading.

Know how much work is entailed in the refinishing of an

object and what constitutes really bad condition.—Pieces "in the rough," that are in need of refinishing, are the best buys in antiques. Therefore, you cannot expect these things to be in excellent condition. But you should be aware of what is needed to put them into good condition. If it is just refinishing, fine—but when you get into cabinet work, there are things which make an object just too much of a project for an amateur and still other things which make an object's revamping questionable for anybody. If the cabinet work involved is just gluing, you will probably be able to do it, but if it is more involved, you may not have the facilities. If the object is a real bargain, it might be worth your while to have a cabinet-maker do the cabinetwork for you.

Serious problems are: a crack or break at a crucial joint, or, a piece which has a section or sections, such as a chair seat, riddled with cracks and gouges which have been filled with plaster. I came home with a rocking chair in the latter category one time. It had many layers of paint covering it, and there was nothing to do but to give it another, instead of the natural finish which I'd planned.

The most serious problems of all are termites and rot. If a piece has had these in any quantity, forget it! You can test for termites by tapping the wood. If the sound is hollow, or if you see any residue of saw dust, beware!! Rot is easily detectable because the wood is soft and spongy. You can drive a knife, or even a pencil, into it easily.

Know what things should cost.—Antique prices vary considerably from place to place. Geography, particularly, creates a variance. New England antiques are usually cheaper in New England and Pennsylvania ones in Pennsylvania. This makes sense. But pieces may even differ greatly within a locality and this is for the most part due to either the ignorance of a dealer, which can make for a bargain, or to the slyness of a dealer, who sees in an object a chance to get more than its real worth from an overanxious buyer.

In order for you not to be this overanxious buyer, you should have an idea of a reasonable price for an object before you buy it. There are many good antique books which give the price ranges for every piece they discuss. Ormsbee's *Field Guide*, which I mentioned earlier, is one of these. There are other books which simply list thousands of items and their current prices. These act as good guides, but I've found their prices to be quite high for the areas I frequent. The reason for this is probably because their figures are based on antique prices throughout the country, and admittedly the East has the best treasures. Also, city antique shops are usually far and away more expensive than country ones, although you ought not to be afraid of "fancy-looking" antique shops. Sometimes they have better prices than their shabby colleagues who, with a knowledge of psychology, capitalize on this shabbiness by jacking up their prices for those people who think they must be getting a bargain in such a "junky" place.

While using books as references and guides, you should also do some comparative shopping in your area. Go to antique shops and inquire about the prices of as many articles as you comfortably can. Ask about pieces which you are not actually interested in as well as those which you are. These prices will serve as useful references later.

Once you have a good idea of the prices of some key pieces of furniture, you can then use them as gauges to judge whether a shop's prices are reasonable or not. This is usually quite reliable although not infallible as a dealer can have some reasonable prices while having others which are outrageous.

BUYING IN AN ANTIQUE SHOP

Many beginning antique buyers are not aware that, unlike other shops, antique shop prices are not firm. The prices marked on the furniture or quoted by the dealer are the *starting* prices—the price the dealer in his most optimistic moments thinks he might get from an unquestioning novice, but not the price he is willing to settle for. Thus bargaining is an important part of antiquing. This appals some people's sensibilities, but it's true. You don't have to be brazen about it, just ask a dealer of an object, "What is the best you can do

on that?" This establishes you as an experienced antiquer,
one who knows that the marked price on an article is merely
a formality. If the price he then quotes still seems too high,
tell him so and mention the price you would be willing to
pay. He will probably grimace and say he had to pay that
much to start with (which may or may not be true) and
couldn't possibly let you have it for less than such and such,
which will be somewhere between his second figure and
yours. If the dealer seems adamant and the figure reasonable,
fine. If not, turn your back on it and the dealer may or may
not come around.

Suppose you find a piece which, though a good buy, is
more than you can afford at the moment. It is, however,
something you know you will not be able to find again, and
you want it desperately. I hesitate to say this because it
would be wise only after much deliberation and under certain
circumstances, but antique dealers in particular are very
obliging about holding an item for a customer for a small
deposit. One of our prized possessions is a Swedish court
cupboard. It is very old, 1690, and we found it in an antique
shop early in our married life. We wanted it—oh, how we
wanted it! We were sure of its authenticity and its price,
after some haggling, was a real bargain. But it was far more
than we could afford as a lump sum at that time. We knew
we'd never find another one because checks with antique
books disclosed that these were to be found mainly in museums. After much thought and planning, we gave the antique dealer a small deposit, delightedly watched him write
SOLD in big bold letters across our prize and sent him small
amounts every month until the end of the year when it was
ours, and we triumphantly brought it home.

The difference between this and charging (which as you
should know by now I think is to be avoided if at all possible
by newlyweds) is that you are not obligated to a certain
amount at any specific time. The very fact that you don't
take the item until it is paid for makes you pay for it just as
fast as you can. Antique dealers know this, and a reputable,
sympathetic one will be delighted to "help out the newly-

weds" with this service. Use this device only after careful consideration, though, and be careful not to commit yourself to a sum which will be difficult to realize.

I have been talking mainly about furniture and you may be wondering about dishes, lamps, glass, pewter, copper, etc., also. Some of the same rules, such as knowing your dealer, knowing what things should cost and knowing your periods, apply to all antiques; furniture and *objets d'art* alike. But these other objects have their own special characteristics and tips. It would be well to read about them in specialized books before venturing forth on their pursuit.

BUYING AT AUCTIONS

One of the best and one of the most entertaining places to get antiques is at auctions. Those of you who have never been to an auction have a treat in store. They are fun and not nearly as mysterious as some people suppose.

There are several different kinds of auctions. At one end of the scale are the auctions in fashionable city galleries, where the effects and treasures of wealthy and famous people are sold in a dignified manner to a seated hushed crowd. At the other end are the folksy country auctions where people excitedly cluster around a hoarse, gesticulating auctioneer mounted on a tree stump, table, or any other handy object, enthusiastically selling his wares, while admonishing Jane Doe that her husband "wouldn't want her to pass up the garden hose at such a ridiculous figure" and encouraging Mary Brown to "go ahead and buy the patchwork quilt, 'cause it will keep you and Harry warm, come winter." "Believe I would!," he encourages, as she hesitates. It is this kind of auction, with its lunch served by Ladies' Aid Societies, which is so rewarding to the bargain hunter. Since the good ones are now attended by dealers, the yield is not as fantastic as it once was, when a drop-leaf cherry table went for a dollar, but treasures are still to be had. After all, even if you are bidding against a dealer, you can still get a bargain. He obviously can't pay as much as he'd ask in his shop.

These auctions can be the result of an elderly couple's leaving their farm for a smaller apartment and selling a motley collection of things, ranging from farm implements to a deep freezer, to a few antiques, or it can be an antique shop going out of business, which will be a fine sale, but will also draw a large crowd of people just like you, looking for bargain antiques. Obviously, the more antiques a sale has to offer, the more antiquers will be there. But don't let this discourage you—they want bargains, too.

You can find notices of auctions and a partial list of their offerings in local newspapers. Rural weekly newspapers usually have the best listings, but daily papers have them too, and some city newspapers have a section in their classified section, headed *Sales & Auctions*. Usually this last is mainly for the gallery auctions which, although not so much fun and usually not within the price range of the budget-minded, are interesting and occasionally yield a real bargain, simply because an item is not of particular interest to those in attendance. For instance, I recently got a pile of what turned out to be thirty-five paneled walnut shutters for $5.00 because none of the fashionable clientele was disposed to carry out a tremendous filthy pile of undetermined lumber to their waiting limousines.

Besides newspaper notices for auctions, you will find placards in store windows of a small town about their auctions, antique shops will sport notices, and one auction will usually have "flyers" for others. The auctioneer of a country auction may also announce somewhere in his spiel that, "next week we'll be over at Hannah Low's place selling some dandy things." Once you get started in the auction circuit, you can usually be entertained regularly for most of the season, which in the East is at its best in the spring and fall.

Before you consider buying anything at an auction, you should of course know the same things about antiques that you need to know for "antiquing" in a shop. Besides these things, you should know the actual mechanics of an auction, which though second nature to a seasoned auction-attender, are confusing to a "first-timer."

When you arrive at the auction site, which, let's say is a house in the country, you will probably see furniture everywhere—on the lawn, on the porch, and the people milling in and out will suggest there is more in the house. Do as the milling crowd is doing; wander around and look at the furniture to be sold (sometimes the day before a sale is set aside for examination of pieces also, but usually this is not the case for country auctions). Pick out the things that interest you and inspect them thoroughly for wood type, condition, age, etc. Then mentally put a price on these articles, one that you'd be willing to pay (and don't be carried away and bid over this price). Keep this figure and your enthusiasm to yourself. An auction is really a competition and your enthusiasm can be a hint to your competitor. It is hard not to get carried away, but be casual and cagey. The bored, off-hand look found on the seasoned antiquer isn't there by chance. It has been carefully cultivated.

When "your" article is finally put up for bid (suppose you are willing to pay $10.00 for it) let someone else start the bidding. The auctioneer will start by asking for an outrageous figure such as $15.00 which he may not even expect to get at the end. There will be a long silence and finally the auctioneer will say "all right, who will give me $7.50?" Another pause. "$5.00?" Still another pause. "$3.00?" All right, what will you start this dandy chair at? Come on, folks, give me a bid!" Finally, someone who can contain himself no longer (this might be you if the wait has been long enough) says 50¢. In mock horror, the auctioneer will say, "Now, really!" But he'll accept the bid and the bidding will have begun. From then on he'll try to make you bid as high and fast as he can, but don't be intimidated—inch up as slowly as you like. If the auctioneer has $3.00 and is asking for $4.00, don't hesitate to call out firmly $3.50. There is psychology involved in auction bidding, and the auctioneer tries to use it, too. He tries to make you feel stingy if you don't bid fast and furiously, but don't let this bother you— you will get used to it. Everyone does.

As you go to auctions, you will learn to use your intuition

more and more. If you know someone else is particularly interested in "your" piece, sometimes it's advantageous to "jump" his bid (that is, if the bidding has gone up a dollar a time and your opponent has just said $3.00, say $5.00 instead of the $4.00 bid which is expected from you) hoping this will discourage him into forgetting the whole thing. But in the beginning, it's well to go up firmly, but slowly, and stop when you get to what you should have previously decided is your limit.

It is easy in the excitement and competition to think, "Just one dollar more and it will be mine." This can go on forever, and when you finally get the item you limply think, "What have I done?" So be firm with yourself. A little tip—most people set their top price at a round figure, say $1.00 or $15.00, so set yours somewhere in between, $11.00, maybe. This way you won't have as much reason to worry that Molly Brown may have got that gorgeous vase you wanted so badly on what was her very last bid.

If you cannot stay until the end of an auction and there is an item you are interested in, and it looks as if it will not be put up for some time, you can ask the auctioneer if he will put it up as soon as possible. He will usually be very obliging and auction it within the next few minutes. You may feel you should start the bidding on this since you had it "put up," but don't feel you have to go any faster or any higher than you normally would, and feel perfectly free to stop any time you wish. This accommodation is nice to know, but if you can, avoid using it to bring out "your" item at the peak of a sale while the biggest crowd is there. People come and go at an auction and about half way through the crowd is the largest. It is only logical that at this time the prices usually go the highest. I have got my best auction bargains toward the end of a sale, so try not to be in a hurry.

REFINISHING FURNITURE

□

TO REFINISH OR NOT TO REFINISH

FIRST, a word of restraint about the refinishing of antiques. When you first catch the antiquing and refinishing bug, it is a common fault to want to refinish *everything*. You get in the habit of thinking about every piece you see, "It will be lovely when refinished." You just can't bear to leave anything alone.

Gradually, though, you learn that some old finishes are better left as they are, or at most revived. If you have a piece with really early paint, for instance, even though it is rather worn, consider simply washing and waxing it instead of removing the paint. This old paint is part of the atmosphere of the piece and in removing it you will remove much of the atmosphere and, incidentally, some of the value.

Friends of ours learned this the hard way when in their early enthusiasm for refinishing, they painstakingly stripped down to the bare wood an old blanket chest only to discover later that what they'd removed was early American blue paint. Such paint is seldom found on pieces and when it is, it enhances their value greatly. By the time our friends discovered their *faux pas* they had mellowed sufficiently in their tastes (changing tastes again!) to realize that painted pieces can be equally as charming as natural wood ones. Now they would give anything to bring back the paint on their chest, but, alas, it is gone for ever.

The Swedish cupboard I mentioned in an earlier chapter, was saved from such a fate, only because we felt it deserved an expert furniture refinisher to remove the old green paint. Fortunately we couldn't afford an expert at the time and by the time we could, we had discovered the charm of painted furniture as a foil to natural pieces and knew that our cupboard would loose much of its charm along with the paint, and that without it, it would be just another piece of pine furniture.

If you have purchased such a piece, consider for a while before attacking it. You can always remove old paint, but you can't put it back.

If the paint is patchy and quite worn in spots, you can "rearrange" it for a more uniform effect by first cleaning the surface of grime and old wax with naptha, benzine, or even a strong household detergent, applying some liquid paint remover, and with a nonabsorbent cloth ease some of the loosened paint into the bare areas.

If you have decided that your piece bears neither old paint nor a good antique patina (that is the mellow look acquired with age from long usage and countless polishings and something that most certainly should be preserved), continue the chapter.

As with most of the rather technical material in this book, there are many good and detailed books on all kinds of furniture refinishing and cabinetwork which you should look into before undertaking an extensive project. But it seems only fair, after having recommended so strongly this kind of do-it-yourself project, that I describe the methods which, after trial and error, we have found to be most satisfactory.

Keep in mind, however, that the methods described here are not the ones to be used on really fine old furniture. Such furniture needs special treatment and should be tackled only after considerable experience. In the meantime, better turn it over to an expert.

THE FOUR STEPS OF REFINISHING

Basically, there are four steps to furniture refinishing. They are: removing the old finish, doing any necessary cabinet or repair work, (Actually these two steps are sometimes reversed—one school prefers to refinish first as they claim that this way glue joints are not loosened by the refinishing—also this school sometimes takes a piece apart to refinish it then puts it back together, carefully gluing all the joints and doing any necessary cabinetwork. The other school does the cabinetwork first, as they say in removing the old finish, residue gets into the joints and cracks which makes it impossible to get a firm glue joint. So be it sufficient to say both procedures are used and you will have to use your own judgment as to which is best for the particular piece you're doing), sanding and smoothing the exposed surfaces and, finally, applying the new finish.

REMOVING THE OLD FINISH

Occasionally you will find an old piece which has simply been waxed through the years and there is a messy combination of layer upon layer of wax and dirt. This "finish" of course, is the easiest to remove; naptha, benzine, or a household detergent and a Turkish towel or brush will do the trick and you are left with the lovely natural patina of antique wood.

The other finishes are a bit more difficult to remove. The majority of old finishes are either varnish or paint, but some pieces have a shellac coating and still others, heaven forbid, have coats of all three.

For maximum efficiency try to decide what the finish is. You can do this by testing a small area with the various solvents of the common finishes.

Certain preparations work better on some things while there are others which are more efficient for others. For instance, shellac has an alcohol base, so denatured alcohol is the best remover for it. Use a sponge or fine steel wool.

We recently discovered a method for removing varnish which works like a charm. As yet the only fault we can find with it is that the wood gets rather wet which sometimes tends to loosen the glue. The method is simply household ammonia and steel wool. Pour a little bit of ammonia on the article which you are working on and then rub it in with steel wool. The ammonia dissolves the varnish, resulting in a muddy liquid which you wipe off with a damp cloth. Do a smallish section at a time and the results are remarkable. Furthermore since the wood isn't actually scraped, the smoothing of it is very easy too. This is also a good method for removing oxidized paint—if you must—but do use it out of doors as the ammonia fumes are rather overwhelming.

There are special commercial preparations for both varnish and paint removing. Some of the preparations are specifically for paint but most of the new ones can be used for both. These are good since often there is varnish under a paint finish. Follow the directions on the can and pay special attention to the length of time advised for penetration of the remover before you begin to scrape. If you are overanxious and don't let the remover "work" long enough, it doesn't have a chance to loosen the old finish properly. Conversely, if you let it sit too long, the whole mass will reharden and you will lose much of the effect and have to start all over again. A good method, and timetable, for most removers is to apply one coat of remover, wait fifteen minutes, apply another coat, wait another fifteen minutes and then begin scraping.

If there is a thin layer of finish, which unfortunately isn't often the case, you may be able to effect its removal with a scrub brush, steel wool, and either water or an appropriate solvent. Usually it will require a bit more effort.

A paint scraper is good for large flat surfaces. These are too cumbersome for small, detailed, or irregular sections, such as carved chair legs and rungs, etc., though. For such surfaces, we use the sharp edges of bits of broken glass (some experts shudder at this treatment, saying that it cuts the wood, but we've never had any damage from it). Any flat glass which has been broken, or will break into manageable pieces with flat sides, will do fine. Use it as you would a scraper—with long, deft strokes *with the grain of the wood,* applying as much pressure as you need. Use a piece until it begins to get dull, then turn it to another side or get a new piece. Beaded, carved, and turned sections present a special problem. If bits of finish remain on these, go over them with alcohol and a clipped paint brush (this is an ingenious device of a well-known New England cabinet-maker and consists of a one-inch paintbrush which has had about one-third of its outside bristles clipped off two-thirds of the way down—allowing for a good "scrubbing surface.")

Emery cloth is also good for small surfaces, particularly chair rungs. For these you can tear it into strips which can be pulled back and forth in much the same manner as a shoe-shine boy uses his cloth.

If stubborn bits of paint or varnish persist, they can sometimes be removed by daubing them with a coat of high-grade white shellac, thinned with 25 per cent to 35 per cent denatured alcohol. Let this dry twenty-four hours, then use remover on it and the paint or varnish should come off with the shellac.

Really stubborn finishes can be removed with lye. The best lye mixture we've found is one can of lye to one box of cornstarch to one gallon of water. Mix the cornstarch and water first and then add the lye. The lye "cooks" the cornstarch, making a gelatinous mixture which clings well to the furniture. Apply it liberally with a paintbrush. Don't be dainty; literally slop it on. And use rubber gloves. This stuff is potent. If you should get any on your skin wash it off with lots of cool water. Let the mixture stay on the furniture for about eight to ten minutes. Test before the time limit, because if it's left on longer than necessary it will burn the wood beneath. Remove the mixture with a stiff brush and water. After it's all off, wash the piece well with water and then neutralize the wood with a mixture of about one part vinegar to three parts water.

This technique works beautifully; it removes finishes completely when nothing else will. My mother discovered it after she had been working on and off for a year on a spool bed. The bed had six coats of different colored paint which nothing seemed to penetrate and getting down into the spools was almost impossible. Then a woman told mother about the lye treatment. She used it, and had the bed completely stripped in an afternoon. But the method is tricky. As with the bed, it can work quickly and beautifully, but it is strong and if left on too long it can burn the wood, causing blotches and stains, which are next to impossible to remove. This happened to us once with some little maple chairs. So use this method only as a last resort and then be careful to let the lye stay on only long enough to penetrate the finish—not the wood, and then neutralize carefully. Also, read the lable on the lye can, because it is dangerous if used improperly.

CABINETWORK

Except for simple gluing, the next step in furniture refinishing, is so diversified and specialized as to require a complete book if you even hope to touch on some of the problems you might encounter. A good book on restoring antiques is: *The Complete Book of Furniture Repair and Refinishing* by Ralph Parsons Kinney.

SMOOTHING OF THE SURFACE

After you have removed all traces of the old finish and done any necessary cabinetwork, you are ready to prepare the wood for the new finish.

Although frowned on by the purists, the biggest boon to the refinisher is the electric sander. These, used on the large flat surfaces of a piece of furniture, cut its refinishing time in half, and if used carefully and always *with the grain,* (that is, in the same direction as the grain,) you will have a beautiful job. Don't, however, try to do small rounded or carved places with the electric sander because you will pare down the carving and flatten the rounded surfaces before you know it.

If you are planning on much refinishing, you should consider buying your own electric sander. Sometimes you can get a good buy on them at auctions and sales. If you aren't inclined to make such an investment, electric sanders can be rented by the hour or day for a small fee from most lumber yards and hardware stores. In some cities there are stores which actually specialize in renting carpentry, garden, and house-cleaning tools. (As an aside, floor polishers can also be rented at these stores and they are a great help, particularly when you first move into a place.) When either buying or renting an electric sander, be sure not to get a disc sander, as with this type of sander it is impossible to sand with the grain since the disc moves in a circle. This is also why your electric drill won't work as a sander.

An electric sander used with a felt belt and pumice and oil may also be used for a final polishing.

You will have to do small, rounded surfaces by hand. Emery cloth can be used for these since it will bend to fit the contours of the piece. But another gimmick preferred by some is to dampen the back of a piece of finishing paper to make it pliable and crumple it into a ball. Then by using your hand or fingers as a sanding block (that around which you wrap the sandpaper) you can get into the crevices quite well.

"When you think you have thoroughly sanded a piece, sand it some more" was the rather vague, discouraging advice given to us, when we first began refinishing furniture. What this advice means is—you may think that a piece which feels smooth to the hand is ready for its finish, but this may not be the case. With prolonged sanding, wood can become more than just smooth-feeling; it can acquire a smoothness which is akin to satin. It fairly glows and is so smooth as to actually have mirror qualities. It is this surface for which you are striving, indeed, which you need, to have a really beautiful finish. Most finishes will tend to raise the grain slightly, making the result not quite as smooth as you had thought, therefore just a "fairly" smooth surface may end up almost rough. This raising of the grain is almost imperceptible with most hard woods, but with soft woods it is sometimes evident enough to dictate deliberately wetting the smoothed surface before applying the finish in order to raise the grain, which is then sanded down again.

Whether hand-sanding or using an electric sander, remember to stay with the grain. I can't stress this often enough. Sand with quick uniform strokes, not staying in one place too long. After smoothing as well as possible with three grades of sandpaper (medium coarse, medium, and fine), either by hand or machine, a final polish can be made with oooo steel wool (the finest steel wool) and/or with pumice, which can be bought in a powder and used like a cleansing powder with a cloth dampened with water or rubbing oil.

APPLYING THE NEW FINISH

Now comes the most fun of all, applying the finish. Up to now, it has been relatively tedious work with little visible results. All of a sudden with this final step, all the fruits of your labors are gloriously realized.

Many antiques boast several woods in one piece since woods were used which adapted themselves best to a particular function; for instance, hickory, because of its strength, was often used for legs and spindles of chairs. Your first inclination may be to stain the wood to conformity but consider this first: wood loses it natural highlights and natural glow when stained and often the inclusion of several woods in one piece can be quite attractive and will act as a "tying agent" if you have several kinds of wood in your home.

Some people like to use a filler preceding the finish—particularly on open-grained wood—but fillers are tricky to use and many good cabinet-makers feel they are not necessary, or in fact desirable, since they claim, if you look carefully, they are always visible.

A filler, as its name implies, fills the cracks made by the grain. There are commercial fillers for sale which you rub into the wood, let the grain absorb and then rub off. These come two ways, colorless and in wood-stain colors. If you use the colorless fillers preceding an oil finish the result will be white hairlike lines since the grain is filled with the filler and its color will not be changed by the oil as will the wood's. This is particularly noticeable on a dark wood such as walnut but even a light wood such as pine will darken with age while the filler will not, hence, the stained fillers. Stain has always been more or less a dirty word to me, so I would definitely avoid these; however some of my friends have used them to advantage. An alternative is the use of shellac as a filler, if you want one. This you apply by wiping on orange shellac with a cloth *across* the grain of the wood, then wiping it off *across* the grain while still wet, with a dry cloth. This process fills the grain without getting a thick layer of shellac over the entire piece. The surface should be sanded or steel-wooled when it is completely dry.

Whether or not you use a filler will depend on your experience and your own preferences. Apply a little bit of a finish to an inconspicuous place on your piece first and if you like it without a filler, fine.

Natural Finishes

The easiest natural finish, and my favorite is a linseed oil one. The application of the oil turns the wood the lovely glowing color which you associate with that particular wood and the effect is rich, but natural.

Linseed oil can be bought at virtually all hardware, paint and five-and-ten-cent stores. But be sure you get *boiled* linseed oil, or your finish may be tacky, with the oil never quite drying.

Before applying the oil (or the filler if you are using that first) be sure your surface is absolutely free of dirt or sanding residue. Go over it carefully with a cloth and then with your hand or a damp cloth.

The oil should be diluted with turpentine, one-half oil to one-half turpentine. Sometimes you can use two-thirds to one-third for the first coat and then further dilute subsequent coats. The purpose of the dilution is to guard against stickiness or tackiness—which can also result if the wood is soaked with too much oil. Apply the oil with a soft cloth and rub it in well with the grain of the wood so it penetrates the wood. After you have covered the entire piece (undersides too, to prevent warping), go over it with a clean cloth to remove any excess. Wait until the oil is thoroughly absorbed and the piece is quite dry, usually a day or two for the first coat, and then give it another coat in the same way. You may want to give it a third coat a week or so later. From then on, apply the linseed oil-turpentine mixture as you would furniture polish, every few months, being careful always to rub it in well.

Oil makes a soft finish, one that stains and scratches fairly easily, but because of its simple origin, it is also easy to take care of! You can remove most marks and scratches by lightly sanding the damaged spot (with the grain, and easing into the adjacent areas) and then applying more linseed oil. If the scratch is a very light one, dispense with the sanding and just apply a bit of oil to it.

As I said, linseed oil is a "soft finish." If you prefer a hard finish, one that is impervious to water, alcohol, and most scratches, the one we have found to be the most satisfactory and natural looking is, of all things, a finish using a floor sealer.

First, rub in a coat of one-third linseed oil to two-thirds turpentine to bring out the color of the wood. Let it dry thoroughly for a day or two. Then apply a coat of floor sealer or spar varnish. The floor sealers are thin and clear, almost the consistency of water. Apply the sealer evenly with a small brush, *with the grain,* being sure to smooth out all the little bubbles which may collect. Also, as with any finish, apply at least one coat to the underside of a large surface, such as table tops or leaves. Otherwise, if one side is left raw, there is the possibility of a warp developing due to the absorption of moisture on that side.

Allow this first coat to dry over night. Rub the entire piece with oooo steel wool until you have removed the shine. It doesn't take long. You may be upset by the way your piece looks at this point, but don't be alarmed. The first coat actually acts as a filler and goes down into the grain leaving streaks which make the grain rather prominent. This is why you need several coats to bring the grain's cracks up even with the surface.

After you have rubbed down the article thoroughly (you needn't rub down the underside) wipe it well to remove all dust and bits of steel. Apply another coat of sealer in the same way. Repeat this operation: Sealer, dry over night, rub down with steel wool, wipe, until you have at least four coats of sealer. After several coats, the steel-wooling does not bring out grain characteristics, but rather leaves a mellow, dull glow. After the final steel-wooling, use pumice stone and rubbing oil—this can be castor oil, motor oil, etc.—with a burlap cloth. At this point you have, except for a slight shine, a natural finish which is quite impenetrable.

The aforementioned New England cabinetmaker uses, as his standard finish, a similar treatment using either clear varnish, shellac, or lacquer. He uses three coats, the first diluted 20 percent with its solvent, the next two full strength. He then sands between coats with oooo finishing paper. After the final coat he uses the finishing paper, then oooo steel wool and finally pumice and oil. The carvings he wipes with rubbing oil, sprinkles with pumice, and then "scrubs" with his clipped brush.

Painted Finishes

Obviously if you plan to paint a piece of furniture, it won't need as much preparation and smoothing as one which is to be left natural, but it is necessary to have the surface smooth or the paint will be uneven. For a professional job on old furniture, you can remove the old paint or varnish as well as you can with a finish remover, and then sand it well with a medium-fine sandpaper. You don't need to worry about stains or bits of color left by the old finish; smoothness is what you are after. You can actually dispense with the remover altogether and simply use medium, followed by fine, "wet or dry paper," with water as its lubricant, to smooth the surface.

When the surface is smooth, it is ready for the paint. There are many, many kinds of paints you can use, depending on the effect you want: For a glossy finish, there are gloss enamels; for an opaque but glossy finish, particularly if you are striving for an oriental effect, lacquer will do beautifully.

Semigloss enamels are indicated when you want a "glow" but not a high shine. However the nicest glow is achieved by using several coats of a glossy enamel, or one or two coats of enamel and several more of varnish, and sanding with oooo finishing paper between coats, followed by oooo steel wool and oil and pumice after the final coat. Flat enamel is the answer for a dull finish.

Apply the paint according to the directions on the can or those received from the paint dealer. For the best results and durability, you will need several coats, either of the original paint or a coat or two of paint followed by coats of clear varnish.

Many of my friends find that spraying the paint rather than brushing it gives a smoother finish. You can do this with a spray attachment on a vacuum cleaner or with a special handsprayer. Recently paint has appeared in stores in aerosol cans, which although a bit expensive, works very well I'm told.

Many paint companies are coming out with truly subtle shades and Early American colors (one company has even reproduced the Williamsburg colors) instead of the harsh colors previously found on the paint charts. If, however, you want an Early American hue and can't find it, you might want to experiment with mixing your own from some of the basic pigment colors. These colors come in several forms. The most common today are the oil or universal tinting colors (although old-fashioned Japan colors which you dilute with turpentine and fortify with a little bit of varnish are still preferred by experts) which for furniture you dilute with a little turpentine and then add a dash (about one-half the amount of turpentine) of quick-drying varnish.

There are many involved formulas for mixing the pigment colors for Early American hues but basically they consist of dulling such colors as American vermilion for red, medium or dark chrome green for green, medium chrome yellow for yellow and Prussian blue for blue, with umber (some people use raw umber, some use burnt umber) and then lightening with white until you get the shade you want. A tube of umber is useful for dulling any enamel color also. Add it gradually, stirring constantly, until you get just the tone you want.

Two books which contain good advice for mixing Early American paint colors are: *Early American Decorating Pat-*

terns by Peg Hall, and *Early American Decoration* by
Esther Brazer.

Antiqued Finishes

Antiquing, as the name implies, is the application of a
finish which is uneven, mellow, and rather old-looking. The
best examples of antiquing are the effects found on roughly
gilded French furniture of the seventeenth and eighteenth
centuries. If you are striving for a French look, this antiquing method is one of the easiest ways to achieve it.

After stripping and smoothing a piece of furniture in just
the same manner as you would for an oil or varnish finish,
rub a thin coat of oil (one-third linseed oil to two-thirds
turpentine) into the wood. Next, apply a thin coat of paint
(preferably white) either by brush or with a cloth. This you
let "sit" only a few minutes before wiping off. Wipe off as
much or little as you like—you know the effect you want. Let
this dry and then daub on, irregularly and as much as you
like, gilt paint for a rich effect, raw umber for a duller one.
Wipe this, too, so there will be no hard lines and the effect
will be mellow and subtle. When the finish is completely dry
go over it with oooo steel wool and oil and pumice.

This wipe-on, wipe-off method can be used with any
color of paint by itself when a "stained effect" is wanted.
Keep the paint thin. Slap it on and wipe it off. That's all
there is to it. The method is most effective on open-grain
woods as the paint goes down into the grain where it remains
a darker shade than that on top of the grain which has been
wiped off. Therefore the wood's grain is quite visible in this
rather "transparent" finish. It can then be waxed or oiled
as a final touch.

A second method for antiquing which, I'm told by a reliable source, works quite well is: After removing the old
finish and smoothing the surface, dapple on light-gray flat
paint with a wad of cheese cloth. Let this dry thoroughly and
then rub down with fine steel wool. Next, apply a thin
(thinned with turpentine) coat of white in the same way,
wiping the paint slightly as you apply it so as to let the gray
paint show through. When dry, rub down with fine steel

wool or finishing paper, then oil and pumice, and then, if you wish, wax.

For a gilded effect, apply umber or gold paint, sparingly, between the gray and white coats.

SEVEN

BUYING NEW FURNITURE

□

BUYING new furniture isn't so different from buying antiques in that many of the same guides apply. Know your dealer (or decorator, or distributor), know your periods, know your woods, know what things should cost, are factors which apply to new furniture as well as to antiques. But as there are specific things you should know before going into the antique hunt, so are there some others for new furniture. Most of these deal with construction and style, but since all construction isn't visible, particularly in the case of an upholstered piece, some reliance must be put on the reputation of dealers and manufacturers. This brings me to the first point in buying new furniture.

KNOW THE NAMES OF MANUFACTURERS AND THEIR PRODUCTS

A "name" manufacturer has a reputation to uphold and is usually consistent in his quality, so get to know these. Look in furniture and home magazines for the names of manufacturers and then write to them for literature about their products. Many companies put out booklets describing their furniture and showing it in attractive settings.

You can also go to a store, showroom, or home show with actual pieces on display and see them for yourself. Any one place will probably have only a few pieces of a manufacturer's line in stock, but they will have detailed catalogues and literature about the rest.

Style and construction are the two factors to bear in mind when considering the different manufacturers' products.

STYLE

As I've said many times before, you should have the atmosphere you wish to create firmly in mind before venturing forth on the purchase of any piece of furniture. Therefore, you should have a general idea of the style you want based on a study of furniture styles, both traditional and contemporary. But there are fine points of styling which you may not have considered.

If you want a traditional atmosphere, you have two choices in new furniture. They are *adaptations* and *reproductions*. Reproductions are exact copies of antique pieces found in museums or restoration sites while adaptations follow the same general lines and character as the original but are modified slightly to conform to modern living. This last is often true with upholstered pieces as many of the early periods did not have such pieces and *if* they did they were not what we'd consider today as the epitome of comfort. However, some of the restoration sites have recently inspired some excellent chair and sofa reproductions of Early America.

So, if you're a traditionalist, and buying some new furniture, you must decide if you want reproductions, adaptations, or in the case of seating pieces, a complete switch to something contemporary.

If you are a contemporary devotee, and, as such, buying mostly new pieces, there are many different collections and designs to choose from—so it is well to familiarize yourself with the different furniture designers before deciding which collections appeal to you. Once you've done this, be sure that all pieces you choose blend and complement each other. Guard against too many of the same curves and angles—that is, you wouldn't want piece after piece with sweeping circular lines. A few such pieces foiled by ones featuring straighter lines would be less confusing. And as with any furnishings, be sure the ones you choose are in good balance in relation to the ones you already have or will be buying.

While we're discussing contemporary furniture styling it might be well to mention that modern furniture is divided into two divisions:

First, *furniture developed on the unit basis*, that is furniture which comes in sections to be fitted together and used interchangeably to meet a wide variety of needs. Such items include chests, bookcases, desks, storage compartments, and some sofas. These pieces are of the same design and depth to provide maximum flexibility.

The second division is *furniture designed as individual pieces*. These are the pieces which are complete in themselves and have a definite atmosphere of their own. Chairs, tables, and some sofas are usually in this group. While the first category provides a solution to space and storage problems, its pieces lack the character of the pieces which are a positive statement on their own. So pieces of the first division must at least be combined with items of the second.

Comfort must be considered under styling also. Most seating pieces are designed for a person of average size, so you should try any such piece before deciding it's for you. The most beautiful lines in the world won't compensate for an uncomfortable sofa or chair.

Factors in judging comfort are: Do your feet rest comfortably on the floor? If not, the piece may either be too high from the floor or too deep for you. Is there the right amount of slant or are you pitched too far forward or catapulted back? Is the back high enough to support your back comfortably? Are the arm rests the right height to support your arms comfortably? They shouldn't be so high as to raise your shoulders. If the piece is a chair and one you want to use for reading and relaxing, is it one which is roomy enough to "curl up in"?

CONSTRUCTION

The construction of a piece of furniture is of prime importance to its durability and long-lasting good looks. Since the advent of the machine, the painstaking craftsmanship of handwork is gone. This is not to say that there aren't well made machine pieces. There are, but, with mass production, there are also some poorly made pieces. So it is necessary to know something of the materials used and how they are used in good furniture today. Before embarking on the quest, you should know what constitutes good construction and what to look for and ask about in a piece of furniture which interests you. Labels attached to the furniture, literature accompanying the furniture (you will probably have to ask the dealer for this), and inspection of the furniture will yield much of the following information about a particular piece.

Woods.—The same basic knowledge of woods applies both to antique and new furniture. Many of the same woods were used then as now although their appearance may differ slightly due to the patina of age on antiques and new finishes on new furniture. But there are some separate details you should know about today's woods and the ways they are used.

First, you should understand the terms—*solid, genuine, veneer,* and *finish.* When a piece is marked "solid" (walnut, for instance) this means the piece is indeed made of solid walnut. If the label says "genuine," this indicates that the piece is made of a single hardwood, veneered on flat surfaces, and solid in structural parts, such as the legs. Veneer, as used today, refers to a panel of wood which is made by gluing five, seven, or more layers of wood—one on top of another with the grains at right angles the result being a wood "sandwich." The inside layers are of inexpensive wood while the outside wood is of an expensive, beautifully grained variety. Modern veneering techniques in good furniture make for wood which is actually stronger than solid wood and also more resistant to warping. With hard wear, there is a possibility that the face veneer will chip, however. "Finish," on a label, refers only to the stain used on the furniture. For example, if a piece is tagged as having a walnut finish, this means that a walnut stain has been used on another hardwood (the wood should also be mentioned on the label, such as walnut-finished birch, but it isn't always. If it isn't, ask the dealer what it is. He can look it up in his catalog.

The best furniture today is made of well-seasoned hardwoods (as opposed to the soft woods which come from needle-leaf evergreen trees) of which mahogany, walnut, oak, hard maple, birch, cherry, beech, and teak are the most popular. The seasoning or drying of wood is extremely important since wood which is not properly seasoned will warp and shrink badly. This seasoning consists of air drying, which reduces most of the moisture, and then kiln drying. Inadequate drying is not evident when furniture is purchased so again it is important that you buy the furniture of a reliable manufacturer as he will use properly seasoned woods.

In order to know how to care for a particular piece of furniture, you should know something of the finish used on the wood. Has it, as I mentioned above, been stained or is the wood the natural color? Is the finish used primarily a natural one, as with rubbed oil finishes, or does the piece sport one of the new transparent, high-resistant finishes or a novelty finish? In any case the finish should be satiny smooth—run your hand lightly over the surface to test for this.

Joint construction.—The joints—that is, where two pieces of wood are joined—tell much about a piece of furniture. The best pieces use the mortise and tenon joint. This is a joint where one side or end of a solid piece of wood is cut to fit into a hole cut in the adjoining piece. In addition to fitting tightly, the two are glued together solidly.

Other acceptable joints, although not as good as the mortise and tenon, are the dowel or double dowel—dowels are wooden pins which are fitted into holes cut in both pieces of wood to be joined—and tongue and groove—a projecting tongue from one piece of wood fits firmly into a groove in another.

The best joint for drawer corners—and one which all good pieces have—is the dovetailed joint. Dovetailing is where the notched ends of the sides fit into the notched ends of the front and back. The difference between antique and modern dovetailing is, of course, that all dovetailing today is done by machine, instead of by hand.

Cheaper furniture will have rabbeted joints and butt joints. These are methods of placing the wood together and then nailing it. Note that the best joints do not require nails.

If you've never seen these different joints, it is difficult to visualize them so ask a furniture dealer or cabinetmaker to show you the various joints.

Another factor for judging good furniture is corner blocks. All good furniture has these for reinforcement. Their main function is to brace legs in both case pieces and seating pieces. They consist of a triangular-shaped piece of wood screwed (the best corner blocks have screws placed right in the corner—these are called counterblock screws) and glued to the rails. Some are notched to fit, and the grain in the wood of the block should run diagonally to the rail. Corner blocks are necessary in all good construction except where the wood is bent or shaped.

Up till now the discussion of furniture construction has been general. Now it is necessary to divide furniture into two groupings—case pieces and seating pieces—for specific details about each.

CASE GOODS

The most significant details of case goods, in addition to those listed above, are in the drawers. Besides having the dovetailed joints as described under *joint construction,* the best drawer construction features grooved sides which enable the drawer to slide in and out smoothly. The *very* best is a ball-bearing construction which is also rather expensive. There should also be dust panels between the drawers.

Other features to look for in case goods are: A dust proof panel in the back; and finished backs, inside surfaces of doors, and other semihidden areas. Also, the shaped parts, such as posts or legs, should have the grain running lengthwise for the most strength.

SEATING PIECES

Good frame construction for a seating piece is the same as for any other piece. Hardwoods (mahogany, birch, hard maple, and ash are usually considered the best), mortise and tenon or dowel joints and corner blocks all contribute to a well-made frame. A seating piece should also have crosspiece braces or stretchers between the legs to minimize the strain, and, as with case pieces, the legs should never be cut across the grain.

The majority of seating pieces are upholstered pieces and, as such, have further construction features for you to worry about. As I said in the beginning of the chapter, many construction features are hidden under the upholstery. Besides relying on the reputation of the manufacturer to give you good value on these hidden features, you should look for the National Association of Furniture Manufacturers new "Seal of Integrity" on your piece.

The following are the features which make up traditional upholstered furniture. (Some contemporary furniture has this construction also but with others advantage has been taken of modern materials and styling to simplify the process or abandon it altogether.)

First comes the frame. Next there is a base for the springs. The best spring support is made from tightly woven jute, three to four inches wide, which is interwoven about an inch apart. On this base rest the springs which should be made of enameled high-tempered steel wire. They should be hand-tied, with hemp twine, eight times each in four directions (four is enough if there is an edge wire all around the seat frame). This tying is what keeps the springs in place and prevents sagging.

There are methods of seat construction other than the webbing and spring type just described. Rubber webbing, rubber covered wire loops and resilient steel bands are also used and are lighter and less expensive than the first type. Also there is some contemporary furniture which has no springs but instead gets its shape and comfort from molded plastic or foam rubber.

Over the springs there should be a burlap cover which is stitched in place. On top of this is the stuffing; curled horsehair is considered the best while cattle hair and hog hair are less desirable. Kapok, palm fiber, and excelsior are also used, but, if used alone, without hair, tend to get lumpy.

A layer of cotton is used to cover the stuffing and make a smooth surface. Then the *whole* works is covered with a muslin covering and *finally* comes the upholstery. On top of this may be loose cushions which are stuffed and then upholstered. Loose cushions today are, broadly speaking, of two types; "down filled," which is usually a mixture of goose feathers and down, or foam, which may either be rubber or a synthetic. I like the down for its cuddly comfort, but many people find it rather sloppy—you do have to "plump up" down cushions from time to time—and infinitely prefer the crisp, clean lines of foam.

Many states require that upholstered furniture have a label specifying all materials and the percentage of each used. So look for these tags. They are usually attached to the underside of the cushion or seat. Loose cushions are also required to carry these labels.

Upholstery is really a separate subject in itself and is often treated as such by the dealer. Usually he will order a piece of furniture for you rather than selling you the floor model (which, if you like and can get, should be cheaper—after all it's "used"). Then you have your choice of a wide variety of upholstery fabrics handled by the manufacturer or you can supply your own.

When you order a piece you are usually quoted the price "in muslin"—that is, before the upholstery has been added—and then you pay an additional fee for upholstery, the amount dependent on the cost of the grade of fabric you select.

Some people I've known have bought a piece in muslin and then slipcovered it rather than pay the price of expensive upholstery. They reasoned that by saving the upholstery money, they could put more into the actual piece and then have it upholstered later in a truly elegant fabric. "Furthermore," said one friend, "I like the easy upkeep and versatility of slipcovers for now."

In choosing upholstery you should consider—besides cost—appearance, durability, and ease of upkeep. What kind of wear can you expect from the fabric? Has it been preshrunk? Is it colorfast? How is it cleaned? Does it have a soil and stain retardant finish? Will it stretch? Will it crease badly?

Knowing what the fabric is made of and how it is made (generally, tightly woven fabrics wear better than looser ones) will answer some of these questions for you.

There are two broad categories of fibers for upholstery fabrics: Natural fibers, which include wool, mohair, silk, cotton, and linen; and synthetic fibers, many of which have brand names but are generically known as acetate, acrylic, nylon, rayon, and olefin. You should study these to learn the various properties of each. (One thing I would like to mention is that wool, due to its elasticity, is particularly good for upholstering foam rubber, while conversely, linen is not.) Often the various fibers are used in combination to join the best features of one with those of another.

Many fabrics are treated with a special finish that makes them more durable and easier to care for. Besides being waterproof and soil resistant, they make the fabric resistant to wrinkles and help to retain its body, thus minimizing the chance of stretching and sagging. Ask about such a process.

FURTHER TIPS

Now that your head is thoroughly swimming with all the details of new furniture and its construction, there are a few additional points worth mentioning in connection with the purchase of new furniture.

You should see a piece "in the flesh" before buying it; particularly a seating piece. These should be sat in and squirmed in to be sure they're comfortable for you before you even consider buying them. Often it is tempting to order a piece from dealers' literature and photographs, without actually seeing it, but don't. The piece may arrive and be uncomfortable and/or not live up to your expectations.

If possible, you should buy new furniture in the area where you live. Complaints, adjustments, repairs (headaches no matter where you are) are more easily adjusted when there isn't a great deal of distance between you and the source.

Finally, I come to a point which will undoubtedly inspire the wrath of the furniture dealers who see it; but this is a book for you the consumer, not the dealer, so I must mention that you are in a much better position to negotiate any complaints if you do not completely pay for a piece of furniture until you are sure it's satisfactory. Unfortunately many dealers will turn a deaf ear to your complaints once a transaction is completed.

Usually a dealer requires a third down with any order. Hold off on paying the rest for about a month, then if you have a legitimate complaint the dealer will be much more liable to listen to it than if he has a completed deal.

Having imparted this little piece of conspiracy, I will leave you to your purchases.

EIGHT

ACCESSORIES

Your Decorating Signature

YOUR flair is inscribed vividly by your accessories and trimmings. Without these, your room may be no more than a furniture collection. I have seen would-be lovely rooms "fall flat" because they had no distinctive and interesting touches. Those rooms looked like elegant show windows, but the personal, the comfortable, and the lived-in look was missing.

Everyone furnishing a home realizes the importance of chairs, sofas, beds, tables, and bureaus; unless you are wont to sit, sleep, and eat on the floor, these pieces are functional, practical, and necessary. But many people fail to realize the importance of accessories—pieces whose main function is atmosphere. Often such pieces are passed off as unnecessary and frivolous by conscientious housewives. But since atmosphere and individuality should be major factors in your decorating plans, these "frivolous" items can be some of your most important pieces in the lift they give you and your home.

THE CASE FOR NOT ALWAYS BEING PRACTICAL

Some pieces boast both a practical use and a distinct atmosphere; a carved Italian chest, for instance, would give a definite individuality to your home while being, incidentally, a good storage place for linen, liquor, records, or whatever else you want to "squirrel away."

But some things exist purely for their own charm. These items are commonly called accessories. My mother calls them things "to feed your soul" and some of the best decorating advice I've ever received came from her concerning such items the first year I was married.

My husband and I were cautiously and carefully buying only the most essential things when one day we found a large green bottle in an antique shop. It was a bottle which had been used for shipping rum, we were told. It was about three feet tall, a lovely dark, rich green, and we could picture it beautifully in a corner of our living room. But, it was comparatively expensive, totally "unnecessary" and there were things we really needed which could be bought for approximately the same price. So, after looking wistfully at it for many minutes, we reluctantly, but sensibly, we thought, turned away and started home.

All the way home we talked about that bottle. How elegant it would be, and how we would probably never find anything like it again. That evening, still thinking about the bottle, we told my mother about it, and how we had been so strong and sensible about not buying it. My mother began to smile slightly and with great wisdom said, "Sensibleness and practicality are very admirable and necessary up to a point, but what a dull world this would be if everyone were always practical. Spontaneity and appreciation of beauty just for beauty's sake are important, too, and occasionally you need something just to feed your soul."

We bought the bottle two days later and the spark it added to our room and the pleasure it gave us then, and is still giving us, is unexcelled by any other purchase. This, then, is the sort of deviation from practicality which I heartily endorse. This is the sort of purchase which brings your decorating alive and gives you great pride and delight in your little haven.

ACCESSORY IDEAS

Since accessories are *your signature* and therefore should stem from your tastes, your ingenuity, and the atmosphere *you* want to create, it would be a bit contradictory for me to give you suggestions for them. So let me simply mention some of the things I think of when accessories are mentioned:

Paintings (they may be dollar reproductions from a print shop), bits of sculpture, collections (pieces of brass, copper, and pewter are our passion—colored glass bottles for window ledges may be yours), plants and *their* accessories (I go into these in detail in the next chapter), interesting items which can be hung on the wall (we have a pair of English coaching horns which we mounted on a burlap-covered piece of plywood and hung above the couch instead of a picture), candlesticks (a handsome pair of candlesticks can be used so effectively, in such a variety of ways, that I think they should be one of, if not *the*, very first accessories acquired) sconces, and interesting lighting fixtures.

These are all things which say YOU; which say, "I am decorating my home, not just buying furniture for it."

BUYING YOUR ACCESSORIES

It seems a shame at this point to put a damper on what is essentially the spontaneous aspect of decorating by giving rules for it, but, as you might think, there can be definite pitfalls here, also.

Obviously you can't go around saying about everything you see: "Isn't that interesting, I need that," or "isn't that different, we must have that." You would end up with an awful conglomeration of things and might never get around to getting the essentials, at least not in the way I'm advocating.

So, *how* does one decide when something is a real treasure, and when it is just a useless extravagance, a whim of the moment? You ask essentially the same questions about an accessory as you do about your more conservative purchases: "How can it be used now? How can it be used later?" (Maybe you won't always want a bobby lantern in your living room; but if not, it would be handsome on a patio.)

Will the style fit in with conceivable future furniture purchases? For example, the antique coaching horns I mentioned; mounted on a burlap mat, they blend beautifully with Early American or Scandinavian contemporary, but their appropriateness with French Louis XIV would be questionable.

If there is a color involved, will it be limiting later? For instance, had our green bottle been orange and some time in the future I decided our color scheme were to be primarily soft roses, this might create a bit of a problem. However, it was green, and since I'm very fond of plants, I knew greens would always be a part of our color scheme.

Finally, we come to the consideration of cost. Most accessories are hard to evaluate as to whether they are or are not a good buy. Often they will be a one-of-a-kind item with no basis for comparison. If yours is something which can be compared and evaluated with something similar, by all means inquire around. Obviously you don't want to pay an inflated price if you can possibly help it.

NINE

DECORATING WITH
PLANTS AND FLOWERS

□

THE warm charm created so easily by plants and flowers in your home is hard to achieve in any other way. Some of the most distinctive touches in a particularly handsome house of friends of ours are the stately plants which grace the floor, the lovely hanging ones which greet you occasionally as you turn corners, and the perky gay ones which add a cheerful note to the kitchen. Plants can be the very nucleus of your accessories and, if chosen and tended carefully, can be as important, and almost as permanent, a part of your decorating scheme as your curtains or your carpet. Flowers, of course, are not so long-lasting but seasonal ones needn't be an extravagance and their presence does much for your decor and your spirits.

Plants

CHOOSING YOUR PLANTS

Choose house plants with an eye to the following:

The growing conditions you can offer.—Different plants thrive or die in different conditions. Some need more light than others. Some are extremely sensitive to drafts and cold and some can't stand temperatures above 70°. Some need a moist atmosphere and some are fairly adaptable to average conditions.

Atmosphere you wish to create.—In spite of what some purists will tell you, I think any plant can be made to fit into any decorating scheme by the way it is used and its container, but certain plants do suggest particular atmospheres or periods. For instance, the quaintness of geraniums and violets suggests Early Americana; ferns impart a Victorian flavor, and the crisp, clean lines of a phylodendron, palm, or avocado plant tend to suggest a contemporary feeling.

The needs of your home.—Do you have a stark bookcase which could be softened by some trailing ivy, or a bare corner which could be glamorized by a regal floor plant? Or do you have a porch where a large tub of plants would add charm?

Containers you wish to use.—Is that delightful basket Aunt Hattie brought you from Mexico craving a pot of ivy or a hanging begonia? Or the Victorian plant stand you bought for "a song" at Mrs. Bates' auction, wouldn't it be handsome with a luxurious fern?

EASY-TO-GROW PLANTS

It would be impossible to include anything approaching a complete guide to available houseplants in a book such as this, but for those of you whose knowledge of flora starts and stops with phylodendrons the following list of common, easy-to-grow plants is included to get you started.

Foliage plants

Australian Umbrella Plant—grows into a magnificent tall tree. Has a cluster of leaves on the tips of the stems which form "umbrellas." Adapts well.

Cacti—particularly attractive grouped together in a "cactus garden." Need lots of light, sandy soil, and to almost dry out between waterings.

Cast-Iron Plant—Aspidistra—an old-fashioned plant which thrives almost anywhere.

Coleus—colorful, variegated leaves of purple, red, yellow, pink, or brown—more colorful in sunlight but can stand shade. Very easy to start new plants from cuttings allowed to root in water. Doesn't like high temperatures.

Corn Plant—a large family of handsome tropical plants, most of which have varicolored long, tapering leaves. Will tolerate semishade.

Croton—sturdy, decorative, tropical plant. Multicolored foliage. Likes humidity and sun, but can stand some shade.

Dieffenbachia—"dumb cane"—so called because it contains a chemical which will paralyze your tongue rendering you nearly speechless if you should feel called upon to chew the leaves. Decorative mottled leaves. Likes light.

Ferns—Boston, rabbit's foot, holly and birds' nest are the easiest to grow. Charming—old-fashioned, but enjoying a new popularity. Like a humus soil, weak sun and humidity.

Geraniums—scented. These come with such tantalizing scents as cinnamon, nutmeg, lavender, lemon, rose, peppermint, and anise. Don't need as much sun as those grown for flowers.

Ivy—tree—resembles ivy but grows upright. Is quite attractive and tolerant.

Moses-in-a-boat—an old-fashioned, easy-to-grow plant with boatlike purple bracts containing little white flowers. The leaves are green on the upper side and purple on the under side. Does best with some sun.

Neantha Bella Palm—an attractive, tough little palm from Mexico which does well with moderate light and moisture.

Norfolk Island Pine—a delightful evergreen whose branches grow in whorls and have bright-green needles. It does well if it doesn't have hot sun or temperatures over 70°.

Phylodendron—there are many varieties of upright phylodendron, the giant split leaf being the most popular. Quite sturdy.

Pick-a-back Plant—so called because of its unusual way of reproducing itself—little plants ride "pick-a-back" on the mother plant. Abundant foliage, easy to grow, tolerant of shade, but likes some sun.

Rubber Plant—this is in reality a fig plant. (The fiddle leaf variety is particularly attractive.) It grows very tall, has handsome large glossy leaves, but seldom branches out, and is extremely tolerant to adverse conditions.

Snake Plant—Sansevera—this much-abused plant can weather quite a beating but like all of the extremely tolerant plants, it only *survives* such treatment. Given half a chance it is quite handsome.

Flowering plants

African Violets—a hobby in themselves as their varieties and colors are endless. Bloom constantly. Special soil is available commercially. Need light, but not bright sun, and moisture.

Begonias—the wax begonias of this large family are the easiest to grow and bloom almost all year in average light. They like a fluffy (equal parts humus, sand, and loam) moist soil. Keep plants pinched back for a bushy look. New plants are easy to root in water.

Flowering Maple—maple-like leaves and pink, orange, yellow, and red balloon-like flowers; likes sun, moisture, and not too high temperatures.

Geraniums—many varieties (some trailing). The dwarf types make particularly good houseplants. Like bright sun, loamy soil, dryish conditions.

Impatiens—Patience Plant—blooms constantly all winter if kept in a sunny spot. Delightful red, orange, white, and pink blossoms.

Kalanchoe—a desert plant having many varieties, the most popular of which has a profusion of yellow, orange, or scarlet flowers almost continuously. Very hardy and easy to grow in sun or semishade.

Minature lemon and orange plants—the orange plants bear small, highly decorative, but inedible, fruit. The lemon plants have large, delicious lemons. Both have delightfully fragrant blossoms. To insure fruit, you will have to do the job of the bees and hand-pollinate with an artists brush or Q-tip. Transfer the yellow pollen of one blossom to the center of another. Need bright sun to bear fruit.

Trailing plants

Ivy—of all the varieties grape ivy is best suited to a warm, dry room. (The other varieties need humidity.) It is pretty (quite grapevine like), undemanding, except for regular waterings, and grows very fast.

Kangaroo vine—this native of Australia, with its shiny, notched leaves grows fast and is tolerant of shade.

Phylodendron—there are well over two hundred varieties (some upright) of this faithful tropical plant which grows under the most dreadful conditions but does best with a little sun.

Pothos—resembles phylodendron except for the creamy yellow variegated leaves. It is as easy to grow as phylodendron and a bit more unusual.

Spider Plant—this attractive, hardy plant is another old-fashioned one enjoying a revival. It is composed of a mother plant which sends out shoots at whose extremities plantlets or "spiders" appear, rather like cascading fireworks.

Sprengeri—a lovely, hanging plant with delicate, feathery sprays. Likes humidity, partial sun and temperatures under 70° although it will tolerate slightly higher temperatures.

Wandering Jew—a large family of easy-to-grow trailers with colorful leaves, the most common of which are maroon and green. Can be kept bushy by guiding some vines back into the soil and anchoring them with a hairpin.

Attractive plants from household seeds

Avocado—easy to grow by simply placing the root end of an avocado seed in water. A small glass may be used for this and toothpicks inserted into the seed to keep the top half out of water. Keep the bottom half wet until it gets roots and the top sprouts, then plant it in soil. Don't get discouraged—sometimes it takes as long as two months before it is ready to pot but then it grows quickly up to six feet tall.

Citrus—plant several seeds from oranges, tangerines, lemons, grapefruit, limes, etc. in a pot of soil. Soon you will have glossy-leaved plantlets which you transplant to individual pots. They will not bear fruit but will have aromatic leaves and, if you're lucky, deliciously fragrant blossoms. Need some sun.

Pineapple—cut the spiked top from a pineapple where it joins the fruit. Peel away any clinging flesh and lower leaves to expose stem. Let cut dry a day and then put

it in a flower pot with damp sand. When roots appear
(in five to eight weeks) pot in loose, fast-draining soil
and place in a sunny window where it should have
blossoms and miniature fruit.

Sweet Potato—suspend a sweet potato in a glass of water
with tooth picks, in the same manner as an avocado seed,
until roots form and there is some growth at top. Then
plant in soil.

SOURCES OF PLANTS

You can buy houseplants from "five-and-ten-cent" stores
(large ones usually have a fairly good selection of the com-
moner plants), supermarkets, farmers' markets (a good source
for the old-fashioned varieties), florists (usually florists specialize in flowering plants and are rather expensive), and last,
but certainly not least, greenhouses. This is where the largest
selection of houseplants is to be found. Furthermore, greenhouse attendants will advise you as to the best plants for
your wants and growing conditions. They will also tell you
how to care for the plant or plants you choose and in general
be quite helpful.

If you have a hankering for plants not carried by a local
greenhouse, there are greenhouses which handle mail orders
for houseplants. One such company is Barrington Greenhouses (Houseplant Specialist), Old White Horse Pike, Atco,
New Jersey. This company puts out a good booklet called
The B/G Guide to Houseplants which, beside being a catalog
is quite informative. You can order it from the company
for 25¢.

CARE OF YOUR PLANTS

Besides the special care needed by individual plants, there
are some general growing tips applicable to most plants:

1. A good average potting mixture is 2 parts loam (top
soil) to 1 part humus (leaf mold, peat moss) to 1 part sand;
some plants need a heavier concentration of one thing or
another, but in general this "recipe" is quite satisfactory.

Apartment dwellers can buy such a mixture quite inexpensively from a florist or greenhouse.

2. Provide good drainage for your plant. If there is not actual drainage such as a hole in the bottom of your pot, stones or bits of broken pots placed in the bottom can act as the drainage. Also, there is a commercial soil on the market which is specially prepared to supply drainage for containers which have none, such as large dishes or boxes used as planters.

3. Don't allow the soil to become "caked"—loosen it occasionally with a fork being careful not to disturb the roots.

4. Water your plants regularly, but not too much. The dirt should feel damp to the touch, but not wet. Overwatering may cause rot, so may "wet feet": Be sure your plants aren't sitting in a pool of water which has collected in their outer pot or saucer. When possible, a good solution to this is to place your plants in a tray filled with 1-2 inches of pebbles. This keeps your plants from actually sitting in water; also it combats the lack of humidity problem (which *is* a problem with modern heating) as the water-soaked, pebble-filled tray serves as a humidifying agent for the air circulating about the plants.

5. If your house is very dry, a session in the shower once a week or so is good for your plants. This also helps to keep them insect-free. Be careful that the spray doesn't bear down on them too hard. You can buy a little handspray for large, less portable plants, or use a Windex bottle filled with water.

6. Give supplementary feedings of commercial plant food periodically. Directions for these are on their package.

7. If plant pests should appear, such as spiders or mealybugs, wash the plant's leaves with soap and water. In addition, you may need a commercial spray.

8. If your plants are in a window, move them back from the glass in the winter so they won't catch cold.

9. When roots become crowded and are coming through the bottom of the pot, it is probably time to transplant your plant to a larger pot.

I have barely skimmed the surface of the selection and cultivation of houseplants. There is so much fun to be had experimenting with the propagation and growing of handsome and unusual plants that it would behoove you to read some of the many good books dealing exclusively with houseplants. Most large libraries have a good selection of these. One particularly good book is *The Complete Book of House Plants* by Andree Vilas Grabe.

CONTAINERS FOR YOUR PLANTS

I spoke briefly about choosing plants for your containers. Now let's reverse the situation. It is like saying, "Which came first, the chicken or the egg?" to try to tell you whether a delightful container makes you look for a congenial plant or vice versa. A big old black iron apple-butter caldron bought on a whim at an auction was the inspiration for petunias on my family's front porch. Conversely their large home-grown "avocado orchard" made them look for a brass bucket.

Often a plant's own pot is sufficient. I, myself, like the ruggedness of a scrubbed natural terra cotta pot when its plant is of the same character—or you can paint the pot. Red geraniums in a white pot—charming!

In some settings, with some plants, you may want more special, more refined containers which contribute to a "bouquet look." Then, the simplest thing to do is find a container of a similar size to the pot and place the pot in it. The plant could actually be planted in some of these containers, but it is better for the plant, because of drainage and for the container, because of staining, if it isn't.

Choose a container in relation to the atmosphere of your room and the character of your plant. For an informal setting, baskets, wooden tubs, brass and copper buckets and bowls are charming. For a more formal room you might want to use pottery, china, glass, silver, or some pewter or brass containers. Scout basket shops, antique shops, and pottery shops for interesting "decorator" containers for your plants.

Walnut doors, a gas chandelier wired for electricity, a large gilt picture frame fitted with a mirror, an inlaid Moroccan chair and a little Oriental rug—all from secondhand shops—combine to make a handsome entry hall that is a tribute to its imaginative owners. (Photo: William F. Martinez)

A contemporary Windsor chair, foreground, blends beautifully with its Early American counterpart, a little pine washstand and mirror (the mirror reached its present condition after a bathtub soaking to remove its veneer) and an early brass kerosene lamp that has been stripped of its nickel plate and electrified. (Photo: Henry D. Friedman)

A floor bouquet of rhododendron dramatically demonstrates how living things can be the focal point of a room. The nineteenth-century bentwood rocker is not uncommon in antique shops. Good reproductions are also available. (Photo: William F. Martinez)

Ingenuity is the key word to describe the collection of these handsome but inexpensive pieces. The table is a piece of well-oiled slate mounted on an old wrought-iron stove base. The lamp base saw many years' service as a fence post before it assumed its present role. The wrought-iron Victorian plant stand was reclaimed from a junk pile. Walnut shutters from an estate auction, a small Oriental rug and a wall relief complete the corner. (Photo: Henry D. Friedman)

A hand-carved reproduction, approximately 75 years old, of a Renaissance piece salvaged from a secondhand shop is further enriched by a handsome tablecloth hung as a tapestry behind it. Either piece could be used separately as a dramatic accent in a contemporary room as well. (Photo: Henry D. Friedman)

The combination of a bouquet of rhododendron in a white ironstone urn and a refinished picture frame turned mirror frame adds a touch of glamour to this bathroom. (Photo: William F. Martinez)

A dramatic color scheme sets off this stunning dining room. White walls and shutters and black cotton carpeting are the background for the approximately 65-year-old Italian table and chairs found in a Chicago secondhand shop and painted robin's-egg blue. Black formica covers the badly scarred table top, and the chair seats are blue and black stripes. The brass chandelier, an old gas one, now uses candles. (Photo: William F. Martinez)

An iron gate makes a charming headboard for a bed. It once graced the entry-way of a Pittsburgh town house and was salvaged from the wrecking company by its present owners. (Photo: William F. Martinez)

A bowl of apples flanked by candlesticks are simple but inexpensive decorations for this nineteenth-century cherry drop-leaf table—a charming "first" dining table and excellent side table later. (Photo: Henry D. Friedman)

SEASONAL PLANTS

Most of your houseplants will be "permanent" ones, which are nursed and cultivated toward perfection, but occasionally you may want to indulge in seasonal plants, such as chrysanthemums, azaleas, hydrangeas or poinsettias, which nurserymen have forced into blooming. In season, these can be bought fairly reasonably at flower shops and supermarkets. They usually are spectacular and colorful—a veritable bouquet —and their advantage to cut flowers is that they last longer. You can count on a flowering plant to continue its blooming for two weeks to a month at least, some much longer. Since these plants have been forced, they have usually worn themselves out by the time they have finished blooming, but occasionally, with care and nursing, they can be made to thrive and bloom again. I have a friend who has nursed a florist's Jerusalem cherry (my favorite Christmas plant) so well that it blooms every Christmas. Ask a nurseryman about this.

OUTDOOR PLANTS FOR THE INDOORS

So far we have concerned ourselves mainly with typical indoor plants, since this is where most of us are growing our plants in the beginning. But there are outdoor plants which can be grown in an apartment, and still others which will flourish where there is the slightest suggestion of the outdoors, such as a porch or balcony.

Spring Bulbs.—Spring bulbs are the commonest and perhaps the easiest outdoor plant to grow indoors. They are also probably the most delightful. Your spirits are lifted in spite of yourself by a pot of fragrant narcissus blooming on a table on a cold bleak day in February.

Narcissus, hyacinths, tulips, daffodils, and amaryllis can be planted this way; choose your bulbs carefully, selecting only healthy-looking ones. You can purchase these in the fall from hardware stores, nurseries and even "five-and-ten-cent" stores. Plant them in a pot of light, moist, fibrous soil, preferably one with plenty of humus (any nurseryman will mix up some of this for a nominal fee) about one-half inch apart, except for amaryllis, which need a six-inch pot for one bulb. Have the bulb tops showing above the soil. Hyacinth and amaryllis should have their whole "necks" exposed.

After planting, water the pots thoroughly and store in a cold (40°-50° F.) dark place. Continue to keep damp until there is a show of top growth of about three and one-half inches for hyacinths, about two inches for tulips, and when the buds show for daffodils. They are then ready to be put in full light where they will bloom shortly.

Daffodils and narcissus can be grown very satisfactorily by simply filling a container with bulb chips (if these are not obtainable, aquarium gravel or bird gravel will do just as well), sinking only the bottom of the bulbs into the gravel one-half to one inch apart and then watering well. Store the container and bulbs in a cool, dark place for about two months to allow the roots and about two inches of the plant to form. Then bring them into your living room where they will have good light. Keep them damp but not soaked, and shortly they will be blooming gaily.

Hyacinths may be grown easily and attractively in hyacinth glasses which are shaped so that the bulbs rest in a position where their base and the water just meet and there is adequate space below for root formation. Prepare your bulb and glass this way and then store it in a cool, dark place until the root formation is well advanced and the bud is about one and a half inches out of the bulb. At this point place the glass in filtered light for about ten days and then put it in the strongest light possible in an airy, but not drafty window. Keep the water level constant, and, *voilà!*, your hyacinths will be spectacular.

Lilies of the valley sound difficult to grow but actually are among the easiest and quickest of all bulbs to "force" indoors. Ask your florist or nurseryman for "pretreated pips." These have been kept in cold storage to prepare them for unseasonal bloom. They will be practically all roots, which you should cut off to within four inches of the top of the bulb. Then, place the bulbs or "pips" in an upright position in a bowl or pot, preferably with no drainage (a pot five inches in diameter will accommodate five to seven bulbs), leaving just the tops of the pips showing above the bulb fiber or peat moss which you should have planted them in. Press this soil firmly around the roots. Then fill the container with lukewarm water. After about an hour, tilt the pot to drain away any surplus water. Place the pot near a light window and keep the soil moist.

After all of these bulbs have finished blooming, stop watering them, let them dry out in a dark cool place, give them a few months rest, and you will be able to start all over again.

Annuals.—Probably the best way for an apartment dweller to grow these colorful plants is in a window box. I have never heard of an apartment owner objecting to these and besides being fun to plant and making a pretty picture of your window, they provide flowers for you to cut and bring indoors.

Window boxes may be purchased from your local hardware store or nurseryman. The plastic ones, particularly, are quite inexpensive, or you can make your own. The plants for them can be bought by the basket from nurseries or roadside markets, or you can grow your own from seed following the directions on the package.

Petunias, pansies, bachelor's buttons, and marigolds I've found to be the easiest to grow and the most faithful; they bloom practically all summer. But you may want to experiment with others, too.

If you have a porch or balcony, consider planting your annuals in a big wooden tub, iron caldron, or similar "planter." Strawberry jars, which come in various sizes and have holes cut in their sides for individual plants, also are charming. I like these best, as they were meant to be, filled with strawberry plants, whose shoots and tendrils entwine them with white blossoms and red fruits, but many things can be used in them effectively.

Cut Flowers

You may be shaking your head dubiously and thinking, "A few houseplants, maybe, but fresh flowers on our budget? Is she crazy?" I think this is probably one of the commonest reactions to the suggestion of fresh flowers, at least at any time but the peak of the season, when friends may bring flowers from their garden, or you can grow your own in window boxes, tubs, or a plot donated by a sympathetic landlord. But you don't have to be a tycoon to have fresh flowers or their equivalent periodically all year long. Nature has gifts for you in the woods and fields, winter, spring, summer, and fall, and if you shop carefully, commercial flowers needn't wreck your budget.

BUYING FLOWERS

Buying flowers does seem like an extravagance when one thinks of buying a large bouquet of exotic blooms from a fashionable florist, but by patronizing local markets you can have lovely inexpensive bouquets almost all year. Farmers' markets are a wonderful source for fresh flowers (and house-plants, too). Their flowers are fresh and very cheap. If you live in a city, and can't find a farmers' market, don't despair, flower stands have good buys too. When we lived in New York, my husband would often come home with a bunch of red roses from a flower cart near his office. I found out much later that he paid 25¢ a bunch for them.

Supermarkets are also a good source for flowers in season. One of the first signs that spring is here is the sudden appearance of little bunches of daffodils in the A & P's. The local florist can have some good buys on seasonal blooms too. He also has foliage, such as lemon, eucalyptus, or rhododendron leaves, which are handsome and have an indoor life span of several weeks.

In the dead of winter, in the East at least, fresh flowers are at a premium and quite expensive in quantities, but no florist thinks unreasonable a request for a single flower, and this is my solution to the midwinter flower problem.

I have a friend who is still talking about the time she came to visit me in February, and in the middle of our coffee table, "perfectly blending into our blue and green color scheme" was a single blue iris in a bud vase.

This was the first time she had visited me, and I wanted

our place to be at its best. But "its best" included flowers, and no flowers were to be had at under $3.00 per dozen. The cost of one iris was twenty-five cents and the effect was, well, as I said, my friend is still talking about it.

CONTAINERS FOR YOUR FLOWERS

As you may have gathered, an attractive, but not distracting container will do much toward "making" a flower arrangement. These containers needn't be expensive or elaborate vases. Often, household dishes will do nicely. Pottery jars, glass bowls, old-fashioned wash bowls and pitchers (for very large arrangements), a cup and saucer (for small arrangements), pewter, copper, and brass pieces are a few of the things which can serve as handsome vases.

Obviously, different kinds of containers are appropriate for different kinds of flowers. Think of the character of your flowers in relation to their vase. As dainty pink roses would hardly be at home in a heavy brass bowl, neither would rugged fall foliage be in keeping with an exquisite crystal bowl.

Go over your containers, pitchers, bowls, etc., and keep an eye open in antique shops and at auctions for pretty and unusual holders for flowers—holders which will blend well with your decor as well as set off your flowers.

You should have a container for single flowers (an inexpensive crystal bud vase), a little bowl for clumps of short-stemmed flowers, such as pansies (a pottery jam jar might do nicely), and a tall vase for long-stemmed flowers or leaves (this could be a tallish pottery cylinder made in a neutral color by a friend taking a ceramics course or an umbrella stand or crock for handsome floor arrangements of leaves). An antique shop could yield a little shallow cut glass bowl perfect for floating a camellia or that single flower which outlasted the rest of its bouquet and now deserves a place of its own.

Flower containers turn up everywhere, often for practically nothing, so look for them and collect them. They are important. Also invest in two or three pin holders in different sizes to fit your different vases. These enable you to arrange your flowers securely in the positions you wish and are a must with most arrangements so you will have neither the bunched-together nor the leaning-out look. Crumpled chicken wire is also a good holder in a deep opaque vase.

PROLONGING THE LIFE OF FLOWERS

A little extra time spent in treating your flowers before you arrange them can lengthen their life considerably. Some tips are:

1. Crush with a hammer the woody stems of such plants as chrysanthemums (these should be broken rather than cut from the plant), peonies, and flowering branches so that they will be better able to absorb water.

2. Seal in the "milk" of plants having gummy juices by singeing the end of the stem with a flame and adding salt to the water in their container. Poppies and hollyhocks are in this category.

3. Hyacinths and some lilies, which have hollow stems, should have water run into these stems until it runs out the flower end.

4. Limp-stemmed flowers such as tulips can be strengthened by wrapping the stems tightly in newspaper and soaking them, up to the flower, in water overnight.

5. Most flowers are helped by immersing their stems in as deep water as possible for several hours before arranging them.

6. Slightly wilted flowers can often be revived by letting them stand in boiling water for a few minutes before plunging them into cold water.

7. You might try adding a commercial flower freshener to the water of an arrangement.

8. Finally, if you want to keep flowers at their best for a special occasion, keep them in the refrigerator until the great day arrives. You can arrest the opening of a flower for a couple of days this way. Once you do bring them into the warmth, they open very fast, however.

Arrangements All Year Long

"But you can't tell people *how* to arrange flowers, it is so personal," was the horrified reaction of a particularly talented-with-flowers friend when I told her I was going to talk about flower arranging in this book. I agree with her in part. I think the actual arrangements are up to the individual, but I think for those of you who are not used to working with flowers, it might be helpful to know what is available when and what can be done on a budget with these. I am hoping that you lucky ones who have already discovered that growing things are indispensable to your decor will get a few hints which you have not already thought of.

I am going to divide these ideas by seasons, because, here in the East anyway, they are seasonal. I am afraid those of you in other parts of the country will have to interpret them into your own calendar of growing things.

I have mentioned all the equipment you will need save one accessory—candlesticks. Remember I mentioned them earlier? Well now for their major role. I am exaggerating only slightly when I say I absolutely could not get along without a pair of candlesticks. You see, I always have my most important arrangement on the dining table, often on a mat or stand, but always flanked by candlesticks holding blending, colored candles. This sort of display is simple but, if done with a bit of thought, has an amazing air of elegance and perfection, while remaining homey. It can be used on a side-table, bookcase, or dining table—any place that is large enough not to be overpowered by it. Another candle suggestion—encircle your candles in their holders with little plastic flower holders (these can be purchased in almost any florist's shop) filled with flowers.

Spring.—Spring is a wonderful, gay, and refreshing time and one of the things that make it so special is the sudden appearance, after a long cold winter, of sweet-smelling delicate flowers. Take these flowers into your house and you are taking in a bit of spring.

I spoke of forcing bulbs; these will begin coming up, if planted early in the fall, shortly after January first. Except for these, you will have to wait until about the first of April for most of the season's gifts.

While you are waiting, it might be well to experiment with some more "forcing." Almost all flowering bushes and trees, including fruit trees, horse chestnut, pussy willow, and forsythias can be forced in February and March (pussy willow, jasmine, and a few others can be started as early as January). Collect branches from your friends who are pruning their bushes and trees at this time. Choose the long branches that have an abundance of buds and are not frozen, as frozen branches will not respond. Trim off any dead wood, hammer the end of the stems so that they can better absorb water, and place the branches in deep lukewarm water in a room of about 65°F., with indirect sunlight. The buds should begin to swell almost immediately and bloom within a week or so. They can then be brought into your living room. Keep the tops of the branches from drying out by sprinkling them with warm water periodically during the forcing period. You might also put a flower preservative in the water. The blooms should stay fresh for weeks and there are some varieties which will have lovely foliage later.

All of a sudden, freesias, daffodils, iris, pussy willows and narcissus will appear in gay profusion in the florists, the flower stands, and the supermarkets. Some are inexpensive enough to buy with the week's groceries; others you will want to limit to a spray or two for a special occasion. The longest lasting at this time are pussy willows. They are a marvelous investment. In a tall pottery jug they are handsome; held in a brass bowl by a pin holder (different lengths of course) they can look extremely oriental and if kept out of water they last indefinitely. In water they develop green leaves and the "pussies" become feathery "catkins."

There will also be bargains on potted flowers at this time. Azaleas, begonias, hyacinths, camellias, gardenias, and roses will arrive in quantities for Easter. Buy one of these, put its pot down in a pewter bowl or wicker basket and you have a long-lasting bouquet for your coffee table.

The woods yield all kinds of wonders in spring, also. There you can find pussy willows, arbutus, violets, and feathery branches. Combine these with bits of earth or rich moss and pieces of wood or stones for an indoor wooded garden or use them alone for woodsy bouquets.

Later in the spring there will be tulips and lilacs. Tulips are striking in tall aristocratic arrangements or they can be made less formal by cutting their stems shorter and having several of different colors nodding gaily in a little bowl.

Many people complain that lilacs are difficult to arrange, but I have found that with a pretty bowl, pin holder, some of their own leaves, and the lilac branches themselves cut in various lengths (some quite short), lovely arrangements can be made with them. Trying to fit, willy-nilly, long-stemmed lilacs into a narrow-mouthed container is disastrous, though. Also, remember, lilacs are hard-stemmed flowers and should have the bottom of their stems crushed for water absorption.

Pansies appear late in the spring and their gay little "faces" make charming bouquets in little bowls or jars. If you have access to any outdoor planting area, even a window box, pansies are a good thing to plant. They will bloom faithfully all summer and the more you pick them the more they will bloom. What a satisfactory arrangement!

Summer.—Summer has such a profusion of flowers, to mention all their varieties and possibilities would be impossible, so be it sufficient to say that if you are picking your friends' flowers (by invitation, of course) or your own, do it in the early morning or evening, not in the hot sun, and they will last longer. When you get them home, put them into deep water up to their necks for an hour or so before arranging and then arrange them prettily in an appropriate container, remembering not to have the effect too symmetrical by having an obviously even number of flowers or by having all stems the same length. Flower arrangements should also be in good proportion to their containers—one and one half times the height of the container is a general but flexible rule. In any case, you wouldn't want a few little flowers barely peeking above the top of a large pitcher.

If friends don't come through with fresh flowers, the flower stands will—admirably. They practically give things away in summer. Also, Queen Anne's lace and goldenrod and daisies are just waiting to be picked in the woods and fields. Daisies are some of my very favorite flowers at this time. They are so honest and gay and they last and last and last.

Now when there is such an abundance of blooms, you might want to experiment with drying some of them for the winter when flowers are so scarce. This can be done by placing short-stemmed blooms—face up, please—in a box or can (fruit cake cans or coffee cans are wonderful), covering them with borax, and then sealing the container tightly for a week or so. Or, in the case of long-stemmed flowers such as larkspur, phlox, or status, you can simply hang them upside down in a dark, dry, warm place. These are the old stand-by methods. The flowers are fairly attractive and have a character of their own—that of dried flowers—but they do lose their color. Recently, however, a preparation has come on the market called Flower-Dri. It is a preparation of silica-gel, which dries flowers so they look as if they had just been picked—all the color and form and freshness are still there. The preparation is a bit expensive but you can use it over and over again. The simple directions are on the can. One thing that is not mentioned, however, is to wire the flowers *before* you dry them. They are quite brittle and difficult to work with after drying, but the process is easy when the flowers are fresh. Ask a florist to show you how.

Fall.—Fall is the cozy time, the mellow time, and all her offerings have just that atmosphere. Go into the woods and you will come out laden with gorgeous colored leaves which look so handsome on the floor in copper and crockery jugs, or little purple thistles which make charming bouquets. Nature has dried and preserved cat-tails, swamp grass, milkweed, bittersweet and other field flowers beautifully for elegant, long-lasting bouquets. A Sunday walk becomes a veritable treasure hunt in the fall.

The stores are boasting chrysanthemums in all sizes, shapes and colors, both cut and potted, at this time. They are handsome, inexpensive, and long-lasting. They also have little

pepper plants. Other bargains to be found in the florist's are
the dried things which you weren't able to find for yourself
in the fields. They have cat-tails, bittersweet, mustard plant,
Japanese lanterns, love apples, and silver dollars, all of which
are handsome (silver dollars with their lovely translucent
pods can have a very oriental effect in a contemporary room,
and bittersweet is mellow and charming anywhere), inexpensive (less than a dollar a bunch), and will last almost forever.
I usually regretfully throw mine out in December when I
start decorating for Christmas.

Besides flowers, cut and potted, fresh and dried, there is
another delightful element in the fall. Fruits and vegetables
make lovely arrangements. Ever since the time of the Pil-
grims, people have been using the graceful shapes and mellow colors of fruits and vegetables to adorn their tables.
There is nothing lovelier than a bowl of apples, pineapples,
pears, and bananas topped by multicolored bunches of grapes
(if you have enough, they look particularly handsome in a
white "washbowl"). A basket, bowl, or trough of richly colored vegetables, squash, eggplant, onions, red potatoes, and
ears of corn, has all the handsome hominess of the harvest,
and is a joy to behold. Or, an arrangement of avocadoes,
artichokes, and lemons or an eggplant in milkglass is stunning. Let all of these things have a stint at decorating your
tables before they are consumed. You might have the bowl
of fruit as your centerpiece for a company dinner and then
let everyone help himself for dessert.

Of a more permanent nature, a wooden or brass bowl of
gourds, a little pumpkin and ears of dried corn always get
the position of honor between the candlesticks on our table
in the fall. You can buy gourds at fruit stands, grocers, and
florists, usually by the pound, and, they too, are extremely
long-lasting. They usually go out with the bittersweet in
December.

All in all, there is no excuse for not having your home
beautifully decorated in the fall. There is such an abundance
of lovely colored growth and much of it is yours for the
finding. That which you buy is usually quite inexpensive and

at no other time can you find so much which will last so long.

Winter.—Thoughts of winter decorations are, of course, heralded by thought of Christmas. Every year magazines and books come out with more and more elaborate decorations for "you to make at home." I always buy all these magazines for ideas, but I have found that to try and duplicate most of the decorations is usually difficult and expensive and at Christmas time, like most of you I'm sure, I am on a particularly tight budget for my decorations.

When one lives in the country, limited funds are not a problem. You can always go out, tramp through the woods, and come back laden with the materials necessary to "deck the halls with boughs of holly," or pine or pine cones. But "holly" isn't cheap in the city, at least not cheap enough for great quantities. Still preferring the natural things to the tinsel and Santa Clauses, we usually go to local fruit stands and nurseries and see what they have to offer for our dollar or two and then plan from there.

One year we had a brass bowl full of pine topped with gilded pine cones (you can buy cones gilded or paint plain ones) on a red mat with green candles in our brass candlesticks. Another year we had a pine branch which looked so much like a miniature Christmas tree that we anchored it in a bowl and decorated it as such, with birthday cake candles and little wooden angels. You could decorate such a "tree" with miniature Christmas balls, or gilded acorns, or if you want to invest in one of the wrought iron or wicker tree forms you can decorate these with greens and little fruits, such as kumquats, etc. or with holly.

Still another year our local fruit and flower stand seemed to have an abundance of boxwood and holly. We bought a bunch of each and arranged it with a large pin holder in our large white washbowl. The satiny green leaves and occasional scarlet berries against the stark white bowl was truly elegant. Again, our candlesticks, this time with red candles. We had some boxwood and a sprig or two of holly left over. These we arranged in a pewter pitcher for the coffee table.

A few greens and some imagination is all you really need.

Add to these a splash of color in one form or another and you have a real "creation." One of the most charming decorations I saw last year was a large brandy snifter (any large glass or bowl would do) lined with pine, cradling three miniature red roses.

A variation of the candle-flanked centerpiece which is particularly nice at Christmas time is a 2 × 4 piece of wood, drilled for candles and sporting red, gold, or white ones, heaped with pine.

Fruits are also used beautifully at Christmas. The Della Robbia family of the fifteenth century with their lovely fruit-encircled madonna and child reliefs are responsible for what today are called Della Robbia wreaths. These are made of pine and covered with fruits and nuts, either natural or gilded. Their influence is felt in many other Christmas uses of fruit entwined with pine. A table swathed in pine which is strewn with grapes, apples, tangerines, and nuts, or a bowl on a coffee table, lined with pine and holding apples, tangerines, and nuts (with a nut cracker close by) also have a hint of the Della Robbia family.

There are many special Christmas plants which you might want to invest in also. As mentioned, my favorite are Jerusalem cherries, but poinsettias and cyclamen are handsome, too.

There are also extremely inexpensive decorating possibilities for your door, besides the traditional wreaths, which as I mentioned above could be hung with fruit. You might hang a particularly well-formed branch with little Christmas balls, different colored life savers tied on with colored bits of ribbon, pine cones, acorns, or candy canes and anchor this at a graceful position on your door. One year we found a lovely flat balsam branch, shaped like a perfect two-dimensional Christmas tree. This we trimmed with gold-covered chocolate coins and "planted" in a pot of gold and white striped paper. We then mounted it on our front door, where our only problem was keeping the guests from snitching our "gold pieces."

A door covered with brightly colored oilcloth as a background for greens, sleigh bells, or pine cones is also quite effective.

After Christmas is a discouraging time, an anticlimactic time, and nature doesn't help much. Here in the East at least, growing things are difficult to come by. This is the time for you to use a single flower in a bud vase. Besides iris, which I mentioned earlier in this chapter, single roses, carnations, and lilies accompanied by a leaf or two are equally effective in a bud vase. A single geranium, fuji chrysanthemum, or camellia, also with leaves, floated in a pretty glass dish, is exquisite, and what could be more charming and fragrant than a little clump of freesia in a pretty demi-tasse with saucer!

Your florist should have most of these in midwinter and will be quite willing to part with one of them for a nominal fee. If you are appealing enough he will probably throw in some leaves.

For a centerpiece, you might plant what I call my "tropical effort" which is our table standby after Christmas. This consists of a large glass bowl, which was given to us for a wedding present—for shrimp, I think—(you could use a washbowl, any large bowl or even a large glass or pottery pie plate), filled with "planter dirt" with built-in drainage. I've also used aquarium gravel (if your dish is opaque you could leave the plants in their original pots) and planted with all the interesting varieties of inexpensive plants the "five-and-ten-cent" store has to offer. The tallest plants are in the back, along with an ivy plant, the runners of which are brought to the front and twined around the edge of the bowl. Off center there is a piece of coral and the dirt is strategically scattered with shells and pebbles which we have collected on our seashore trips. This, on a rich brown mat, with white candles picking up the white of the coral, is really quite an elegant centerpiece.

A variation of this is the winter garden for which you can collect moss, ferns, wintergreen, partridge berries, etc., in the woods in late fall. Pack the plants in a box of nursery moss (sphagnum) and keep them dark, cool, and moist until ready to use. Then "plant" them in a giant brandy snifter, apothecary jar, glass bowl or aquarium. Use the moss—green side out—or sphagnum as the "lining" for your container—then add a layer of acid soil. Plant your little plants in a decorative manner. You might also want to try using some woodsy flowers such as myrtle, violets, johnny-jump-ups, or lily of the valley in your garden for a dramatic effect. Keep the garden in a light place, watering lightly—just enough to keep the earth moist to the touch. It should be covered most of the time with a glass lid. The hardware store will cut one to fit. The lid may be removed when there seems to be too much moisture collecting.

Another arrangement for this barren time is one using the flowers which I suggested drying in the summer (or you can get them from the florist and dry them now if you want a long-lasting bouquet). If you have a lot of dried flowers, you could arrange them in an old-fashioned vase as a Victorian arrangement. If you have just a few, mix them with the eucalyptus or lemon leaves which you can buy at the florist.

Fruits are also quite decorative in midwinter. An inviting bowl of polished apples or a purely decorative bowl of lemons and limes are nice on a coffee table. Or you could have bouquets of shining green leaves which are plentiful and inexpensive in florist shops at this time of year.

Don't despair, spring will soon be here.

TEN

SPECIFIC SUGGESTIONS

◨

I HOPE I have given you enough background so that you will be able to give your own interpretations to some of my specific suggestions. These suggestions are ones I have used myself, or have seen my contemporaries use effectively. I think the best way to present these is to take a tour of an apartment, room by room.

The Living Room

Let's start with the Living Room. Living room furniture is some of the most important furniture you will own. It is used the most, open to the most inspection and, often is the most expensive. So it is only logical that you want this room ultimately to be perfect. At the beginning you will probably have neither the experience nor the money to buy these large pieces. Therefore, apply the principles of letting your tastes formulate before buying your permanent pieces and then buy the best of what you are buying.

But, your living room is important now also, so you will want it comfortable and attractive from the start. What can be done about this apparently contradictory situation?

Another one of my premises, as you will remember, is: "Don't buy anything to 'make do' for now to be discarded later, but instead think of everything in terms of what you will use it for now and how it can be used later." That is your answer: buy in reverse. Think of things you will need later, the things for future rooms, the less expensive things. Think how you could use those things as your major pieces today.

COUCHES

A couch or sofa is certainly a, if not *the*, major piece in a living room. Following the above premises, I have found the studio couch I mentioned in chapter two to be the answer. As I said, a studio couch can be used later in many ways— as a couch in a study, television room, or family room or it can be used as a single bed or double, if need be, in a guest room. In the beginning it does beautifully with a gay slip-cover and strewn with cushions (these may be extra bed pillows which can always be used later or now for beds) for a living room couch. It also doubles for the extra bed one needs for overnight guests.

If you want more of a sofa effect than you think the casual cushions create, the whole thing can be streamlined by having one long or two short bolsters in contrasting or matching fabrics serve as back rests. Hang them by ribbons or strips of fabric from interesting hooks or buckles at a comfortable and attractive distance above the couch. There are, also, metal back rests available for studio couches. These attach to the back of the couch and support the cushions.

Other suggestions for your living room couch and what they can be used for later: for a contemporary effect, a long piece of plywood or a door mounted on wrought iron legs with a slipcovered single large foam rubber cushion, or several smaller ones, on "seat" and "back." (The plywood may extend on either side of the cushions, making convenient end tables. This can be used later in all ways as a studio couch except, not comfortably, as a bed.) An antique settle, if fitted with foam rubber cushions, is charming in a "first" living room and can *later* be used effectively in a game room, hall or porch. Some "garden" furniture, rattan and redwood in particular, has large seating pieces which can be used delightfully as "couches" in apartment living rooms, and later you have the most elegant lawn or porch furniture on the block.

CHAIRS

Along with a couch, you will also undoubtedly need a chair or two. Two, I have found is a good number for an apartment. Two chairs add balance to a decorating scheme and make entertaining easier. Conversation (and necks) are cramped when several people are lined up on a couch and one chair. There are all kinds of good, attractive many-purpose chairs which can serve as your living room ones now, before you are ready to get your upholstered "easy chairs."

I mentioned in an earlier chapter one of our pet finds, a Yugoslavian basket chair. This we got for a song, and fitted with slipcovered foam rubber cushions (we bought the foam rubber and cut it to fit the seat and back). It is comfortable, attractive, and has held up beautifully. There are many types of basket chairs on the market, all fairly inexpensive, and all ready to go from your living room to a gameroom or patio.

Again, there are many types of "outdoor" chairs, which today are streamlined and attractive and will do beautifully in an apartment living room; wrought iron with gay canvas seats (there is an elegant circular one to be had), redwood chairs, rattan chairs, and the ever-popular director chairs are a few I've seen used to good advantage in an apartment.

Turning to antiques—rocking chairs and certain Windsor-type arm chairs can be bought quite reasonably, can be made comfortable with cushions, and make a room charming and cozy. They can stay on indefinitely as "occasional" chairs in your living room, or move on to study or bedroom later.

Another idea, and a particularly ingenious one, I thought, was dreamed up by two of our car-crazy friends. In ferreting through an automobile junkyard, they came across two discarded bucket seats. They dragged these home, mounted them on legs, slipcovered them in a delightful print with a flounce clear to the floor and *voilà*, two charming chairs.

If none of these ideas appeal to you, a final suggestion is: Buy your "occasional-type chairs" now. These you would buy ultimately anyway for extra seating in your living room. They are less expensive than large upholstered easy chairs and they will do well as your major pieces now.

Extra seating pieces can be floor cushions. You can make these yourself by buying the foam rubber forms and covering them. Stacked in a corner they make a gay riot of color and are quite handy when you run out of chairs. A bench coffee table or a blanket chest can also be used for extra seating.

TABLES

After seating pieces, tables are one of the first things one thinks of, and a coffee, or cocktail table is probable *the* first, because it is often a coffee table which holds the room together.

Coffee tables

The possibilities for inexpensive imaginative coffee tables are endless. Our coffee table is a large, round, antique table, cut down and refinished to its natural glowing wood. Antique shops yield all kinds of nifty tables and other objects which can be converted into attractive, imaginative coffee tables. I have seen a large, round antique dining table with claw feet, cut down and lacquered black, become the focal point of an oriental-flavored room. It served as a coffee table, and when serving oriental-type meals, a dining table, by seating the guests on floor cushions around it. Small drop leaf tables, also, are very versatile coffee tables. Long benches, too, make handsome coffee tables.

Interesting trays, signs, pictures, indeed anything large and flat, mounted on legs or a stand, can be a unique table. The bases which may be used for these tables are many. If you want to have legs, as such, you can simply screw legs into a piece of plywood slightly smaller than the article used for the top and then mount the top to the plywood. You also can buy ready-made stands for this purpose in many department stores or you can use a luggage rack as a stand.

In the same category as mounting objets d'art on bases, are the offerings of do-it-yourself stores. (We have found the *Door Stores*, of which there is one in Washington, D.C., Philadelphia, New York, and Cambridge, Mass., to have marvelous things.) These stores have lovely table tops in many shapes, sizes and materials. They have finished or unfinished woods—teak and walnut seem to predominate—as well as marble tops. There are bin after bin of the most elegant slabs of marble in all colors and sizes. Then they have legs of all periods and designs which you simply apply in the manner described above.

Or, you can buy a slate slab (If you live in an area such as eastern Pennsylvania which has slate quarries you can go straight to the source and get wonderful buys; we have a friend who recently paid $4.00 for a 2 x 4 piece of unpolished slate in the Poconos) and make a handsome table with it by mounting it on legs or on an item found in an antique shop such as the iron stove base used by our friends. Un-polished slate—often called split-faced slate—is my favorite for such a purpose. You buy it as it comes from the quarry, and simply scrub it and apply a coat of boiled linseed oil. It is slightly craggy (unlike polished slate which looks rather like black formica) which adds interest and it is the most practical table top I know. Nothing hurts it and the only upkeep it needs is wiping, and an occasional coat of oil.

Finally, wrought iron glass-topped garden tables also make handsome coffee tables.

End tables

Many of the suggestions for coffee tables can be adapted for end tables or you could use one or more of the following: the charming little one-drawer stands to be found in antique stores (we have one of these which was ultimately supposed to go in the bedroom for a bedside table, but I can't bear to see it leave the living room), little washstands, or chests, little wrought iron or glass Victorian tables, etc.

You may not need end tables, particularly if you have other pieces such as chests or book cases which offer flat surfaces for lamps, plants, or a cup of coffee.

Chests (blanket or chests of drawers) and washstands

These are good investments for a living room now and infinite purposes later. We have a little pine washstand which is simple in design and has been used as a "table" and record cabinet for our living room, and is now being used as a sideboard and cabinet for linen and silver in our dining room.

Another extremely versatile piece is an old-fashioned blanket chest. Under a window in a living room it makes a table while also serving as storage space. As mentioned before, it can also double for extra seating. A dough tray is still another handsome "table" with storage space.

BOOKCASES

Bookcases are wonderful additions to a sparsely furnished apartment. While holding your books, magazines, and gadgets, they give a room interest and a lived-in look. Our first bookcase was a long, low—two-shelves-high—one, made from inexpensive lumber and painted the same color as our apartment walls. It is now in our study, holding my husband's technical books, and has been replaced in the living room by one of a similar design in walnut (walnut which we bought for a song from a little country lumber mill).

Other inexpensive book shelves can be made by supporting any length boards you wish on bricks, either regular bricks, painted or plain, or glass bricks. These versatile bookcases can be made any height or length you want. I have seen them very attractively "built" at right angles to fit in a corner. They can be moved or changed easily. Terra cotta sewer pipes can also be used quite effectively as mounts for low bookcases.

If you want hanging wall bookcases, there are brackets to be had which you mount on the walls and simply support boards of varying lengths between. These can create a lovely free form, contemporary effect.

RUGS

Rugs are important to make your room attractive, comfortable, and "held together," and they need not present any great problem or expense. Gone are the days when wall-to-wall carpeting was the epitome of elegance. "Area rugs" have now come into their own, and besides making more sense, particularly when one is likely to be moving, they offer far more variations and chances for originality than did the old-time carpets.

So again, think of your rugs as more or less "permanent" investments. The best buy, the one I would heartily recommend for a first, comparatively large, living room rug is a grass or fiber one. They are inexpensive but have a great deal of informal chic. They are versatile (will do beautifully later on as a summer substitute for your wool living room rug, saving wear on this and giving summer coolness. They are also perfect for gamerooms or porches.) They show virtually no dirt and wear like iron. All in all I think they are a wonderful investment. There are many variations of these. While shopping for ours in every conceivable place in New York, we found round ones made in Portugal from flattened olive baskets (these were lovely but quite expensive), some made from hemp, some which came in squares and could be used to make any shape or size rug, some made of woven sisal, and the one which we finally chose. It was made in Japan, and is a type of grass or straw which uses groups of four strands woven in and out in both directions to form inch squares.

Most of the grass and hemp rugs come in natural shades, varying from a honey beige, to a tan with a gray-green cast. The sisal rugs, however, come in a multitude of rich colors.

If you want a large wool rug from the start, carpet stores have large "remnants" which may be had quite inexpensively. These can be a good investment if you consider the three key factors in buying a rug: the fiber content, pile density and height, and workmanship. *Consumers Reports* have long discussions of these attributes periodically.

My third suggestion for a large rug, and one which I hesitate to mention since it violates my principles of buying the "best" and making everything an investment, is a way to have a large "luxurious"-looking rug for approximately the price of two cleanings for a wool rug of its size. Since it is so inexpensive and its effect can be so good, I'll stick my neck out and tell you about our first living room rug. It was a 9 x 12 shag rug bought in the "five-and-ten-cent" store for

$12.95. Laid over a thick but inexpensive rug pad ($6.95), it stayed flat with the help of anchoring pieces of furniture and gave the impression of considerable body. It was, in fact, quite attractive. The one problem with it was, being cream-colored, and cotton, it got very dirty very quickly. Cotton soils much easier than wool, so if you do decide on a cotton rug, get a fairly dark color. Many laundries have facilities to wash large, lightweight cotton rugs, and will do it for a nominal fee, charged by the pound. These rugs, also, wear amazingly well, so can be retired ultimately to a gameroom or study. While not the best investment in the world, ours served its purpose well.

If you do not insist on a large rug, there are many unusual and elegant small (area) rugs, in beautiful materials, designs, and colors which can be striking in a small living room and move happily to any room in the house later on. These are quite expensive when viewed from a per yard basis, but since they are small, the outlay may be no greater than for a more routine larger rug and the effect may be worth twice as much. I am still hankering for a 4 x 6 rug made from alternating squares of black and white alpaca which I saw in an importer's shop in New York. Since I know of no one who has one, I cannot vouch for the durability of the thing and this of course must be considered, but wouldn't it be handsome in a contemporary living room?

The Scandinavians have some beautiful handwoven rugs which come in all sizes, plain or in striking patterns. Many are reversible, being one color on one side and another on the other. Some importers carry these, but almost any good furniture or department store could order them for you. Many American manufacturers have come out with some wonderful patterns and colors in lovely lush, deep, cotton area rugs which should be looked into also.

Not to be overlooked, even—believe it or not—by those on a little budget, are Oriental rugs. These are a fascinating subject in themselves with their colorful symbolism—the legends behind the patterns sound like tales from the *Arabian Nights*. It is quite possible to pick up a small Oriental rug at a reasonable price from an estate sale, an antique shop, or even an Oriental rug dealer. Oriental rugs over thirty-five years old (approximately)—when vegetable dyes were still being used—are usually handsomer than new ones—which have made use of more modern dyes—and as long as you don't go overboard for a collector's item, will probably be less expensive. The beauty of Oriental rugs, besides visually, is that they wear like iron and if you get a good semi-antique one (over thirty-five years old) and keep it in fairly good condition, its value will increase. *Oriental Rugs—a Complete Guide* by Charles W. Jacobsen, is a marvelous book for the study of these rugs. Besides having descriptions and colored plates of hundreds of different ones, it goes into great detail about buying and caring for Oriental rugs.

Finally, for those of you with a real do-it-yourself bent, you might want to consider making a hooked or braided rug for your living room (or anywhere else for that matter). It is particularly fun and satisfying if you can get your husband in on the project with you. I admire greatly a middle-aged couple I know who have a lovely hooked rug in their living room which they made one winter years ago while they were engaged. Following their example, my husband and I are in the middle of a braided rug at the moment. It is great fun and not difficult. There are several good books written which give clear, concise directions for both rug braiding and hooking. The best rug braiding book I've found is *The Complete Guide for Rug Braiding* by Helen Howard Feeley.

CURTAINS

Curtains are one thing which you cannot consider, while you are moving, as an investment. If you are lucky, you may be able to take them from one home to another. But, often, they just cannot be made to fit, so bargains, ingenuity, and creativity are the bywords for these. Disregard the *Buy the Best* premise here (but *only* here) and look for bargains, the major guide being; if they soil or wrinkle easily, will they also launder or be dry cleaned easily?

Most cities have fabric remnant and "seconds" shops, where you can get good bargains. Often fairly expensive well-known fabrics can be had for a pittance. If you have access to a place like this, make a beeline for it. If you do not, don't despair, there are many inexpensive fabrics which can be used most effectively for lovely and ingenious curtains.

Currently, one of the most popular of these is burlap. Burlap is inexpensive, comes in a wide range of brilliant colors, and recently, in plaids and stripes as well.

One of the most effective window treatments I ever saw was in an apartment in Greenwich Village. The apartment had three long, narrow windows in the end wall of the living room. Rather than each window being covered separately, the whole wall was curtained with draw drapes of wide widths of different hues of burlap. The colors in the room were white and mustard, setting off lovely rich woods, and the curtain colors ran the gamut of yellows, oranges, and browns, starting with the palest lemon and working up gradually through the darkest brown. Unless you planned to be in a place quite a while, you wouldn't want to try a treatment as extensive as this because even with a fabric as cheap as burlap, used in such quantities, it would be quite expensive, but a variation of this could also be used to advantage.

Monk's cloth, theatrical gauze, mattress ticking, madras, unbleached muslin, men's suit inner-lining—are some other inexpensive fabrics which can be used with great flair for extremely attractive curtains.

Monk's cloth has a nice homespun look and can be used either plain or it lends itself beautifully to embroidery. Theatrical gauze is good for a light, airy effect. I've also seen different colored threads run through it which was lovely. Unbleached muslin contributes to an Early American look. Particularly in café-type curtains and banded with a little calico print, it is charming. It can also be very effective stenciled. Calico prints, on their own, in an Early American room are of course delightful, too. Mattress ticking, particularly in a blue and white room, can be very effective, either used plain or trimmed with braid or rickrack, red for instance. Men's suit inner-lining is an unusual and very handsome material for curtains. I first heard of it from an artist of some note who had used it in his remodeled carriage house. It is a bit more expensive than the other fabrics I have mentioned, but still not prohibitive. It comes in a gray or beige cast.

Finally, particularly for very large windows, the inexpensive prints found in department store basements can be very effective. Since they are rather thin, the secret for success is to make the curtains quite full, *at least* twice the width of your windows, so the effect will be luxurious and not sleazy.

Wait until you are settled before buying voluminous and expensive draperies.

Unless your windows are a most peculiar size or shape, I would advocate making draw-curtains (easy with pleater tape, which you simply sew across the top) of window sill or bottom of window-frame length, or if you prefer, café-type curtains. They frame your window prettily, draw to cover your window at night and are the most economical.

In the case of outsize windows where traverse rods would be expensive, it might be better to use straight rods and head your curtains with rings, loops or looped tape.

Another charming idea for windows is shutters, hinged together for easy opening and closing. These come unpainted and in all sizes. While a bit more expensive than most inexpensive curtain materials, they can be had quite reasonably from most lumber yards and places like Sears Roebuck. Often they can be found in antique shops too and then they are a real buy. Again, how long you plan to be in your present home will be a deciding factor.

Bamboo blinds are also quite nice and extremely economical. Speaking of blinds, you can make your own and use them instead of curtains. Simply use a gay fabric or wallpaper as the blind, hang it from a blind roller and weight it at the bottom with a pole, stick, or even a yardstick. Or, you can put bands of multicolored braid or ribbon (in your room's colors) on a plain commercial window shade.

LAMPS

Besides being necessary for lighting, lamps can be a very definite decorative asset to a room. My uncle explained buying us a lamp for a wedding present this way: "When we were first married, we lived in a dingy little apartment and the single item that did the most for it was a lovely lamp a friend gave us." Similarly, my uncle's lamp did a lot for our first apartment.

If one lamp so helps a room, two or three will do wonders. Ideally, you should have lighting near every seating piece; the reason is obvious. Three lamps are usually all you will need in a smallish living room. At the moment I am talking about table lamps, but the same applies to floor lamps. Handsome table lamps can be made quite inexpensively from all kinds of unusual and decorative things. I shrink from the too obvious, the things that look just *too* coy and self-conscious, such as coffee grinders, teapots, duck decoys, etc., but some old jugs, newel posts, bed posts, candlesticks, iron fence posts, and other simple pottery pieces can make handsome lamps.

Old kerosene lamps can be electrified for a nominal fee and are charming. They can be found in a host of sizes, shapes, and materials. The colors in the colored glass ones are magnificent. Incidentally, the nickel (silver-looking) ones are always nickel plate over either brass or copper. This nickel plating can be removed by any metal refinishing shop.

Old wallpaper rollers also are enjoying popularity as lamps today. They are handsome and stately and of course their patterns make them one-of-a-kind items. If you can find one at a bargain price, fine, but usually they are rather expensive.

If you prefer floor lamps and want a contemporary look, you might want to consider floor to ceiling pole lamps, too.

Ferret around in junk shops, antique shops, and at auctions and you will be amazed at the field of potential "lamps."

The shades for these lamps will depend on the flavor of the lamp. If it is an essentially rustic lamp, burlap or other rough-textured fabric or perhaps a provincial print could be used. If it is sophisticated, there are many simple, handsome parchment shades and the like in the stores. If it is a kerosene lamp you might want to use a glass shade and chimney in the original tradition or you could modernize it with a fabric shade. In any case (except for the glass "antique" shades, which can be bought in antique shops or reproductions in lamp shops) I have found the best deal on lamp shades to be in the "five-and-ten-cent stores." The variety, the quality, and the cost, comparatively, are amazing.

You can add spice to a plain shade if you like by "slip-covering it." This you do by making a fabric cylinder the size of the largest diameter of the shade (put your fabric around the shade to measure for this), turn the cylinder inside out and stitch the seam. Put the cylinder (wrong side out) back on the lamp shade and make three evenly spaced darts to shape the fabric smoothly to the shade. Sew up the darts, then hem the top and bottom edges. Turn the cover right side out and add trim, such as braid, fringe, etc. Such a cover could be made from almost any fabric, depending on the effect you want—a friend of mine made a most attractive cover from striped mattress ticking and trimmed the bottom with heavy white fringe.

Now, what about the "ghastly" fixture hanging obtrusively from your ceiling? We recently moved in where there was one of these. Again we haunted antique shops and came up with an English ship lantern which replaced it nicely. All kinds of interesting hanging lamps and lanterns can be found which can be easily mounted in place of the current one and just as easily removed when you leave. Some of these old lanterns boast rich colored glass, which does not give much light, but you probably will not be using an overhead light much anyway, and they do offer a veritable "jewel" when lit.

Large kerosene or gas chandeliers are fun in a high-ceilinged Victorian house. Though becoming rather popular, they still can be found in some antique shops for quite reasonable figures and they can either be electrified or used with big fat candles.

Accessories, to which I have devoted a separate chapter and which I recommend as an occasional splurge, will do much toward creating individuality and personality in your living room; they contribute greatly towards making any living room yours.

The Dining Room

Continuing with the newlyweds' apartment, we may or may not find that they have a dining room—an actual one that is. Probably not, in a first apartment, so let's compromise and talk about a dining area, which will accommodate little more than a small dining table and chairs.

TABLES

Your first dining table can be as simple and inexpensive as a card table covered with a gay little cloth—a bit of a nuisance to keep laundered, however. (Incidentally, there are inexpensive table tops available now which fit over a card table and make it big enough to seat six to eight people.) A door or piece of plywood, waxed, or if a stark modern effect is wanted, covered with laminated plastic, and mounted on wrought iron legs, or a handsome outdoor-type table are also good "first" dining tables.

Turning again to antique shops, if your dining area is *very* small, an ice-cream parlor table, and chairs with little cushions are charming. The effect could be quaint or rather sophisticated depending on the color you paint them and your cushion fabric. This group could later be moved to a breakfast nook, porch or patio.

A real prize to be found in an antique shop is the simple little four-legged drop leaf table of the mid to late 1800's. These are easy to find, come in a variety of woods, cherry probably being the most common, and particularly in the "rough" are not very expensive. They are handsome; their wood is usually mellow and lovely and they blend beautifully with most decors and chairs. Since they are rather small (they will seat four to six with both leaves up), their future uses are endless; a side table in a dining room, an extra table in a living room, or a handsome addition to a hall, to name a few. We have one of these and we love it. Ours is cherry and cost $26.00 in a medium-price antique shop. It was covered with all sorts of gunk, but was quite easy to refinish and is one of our most satisfactory pieces.

CHAIRS

Chair possibilities to go with these tables are numerous, too. At first, you probably will not need, nor have room for, more than four. These can be the card table chairs you feel you'll definitely need later anyway, the ice-cream parlor chairs mentioned—either the wire or the bent wood ones, or extremely inexpensive kitchen-type Victorian chairs, painted in a multitude of bright colors to contrast with a white plastic-topped dining table now and later with a kitchen table.

Victorian cane-seated chairs can be had for a song at auctions and antique shops, too. Often their seats are missing, but this can be remedied easily while at the same time helping the blind. Most cities and large towns have blind craftsmen, who do beautiful caning for a small fee. These chairs, though not the most comfortable in the world, are usually made of maple, sometimes of walnut, and are quaint and attractive.

Plank bottom chairs, particularly the Windsor type, are my favorite for first or indeed for permanent dining room chairs. They are sturdy (practically indestructible as a matter of fact), they are handsome and are usually made from a mixture of lovely mellow woods—poplar and hickory predominately. They are quite comfortable, and in general have about them an air of simple, well-made elegance that is hard to duplicate. They are inexpensive and easy to find; every antique shop and almost every country auction boasts a few, so it is just a matter of choosing the style you like best. They make charming occasional or bedroom chairs, as well as dining room chairs.

The Kitchen

Apartment kitchens are often small and equipped and offer little need or chance for your decorating talents. If you are considering an apartment without a stove or refrigerator, I can't recommend strongly enough the advantages of buying used appliances rather than new ones—particularly if you are anticipating moving before too long. Appliances are terribly expensive to move (furthermore you may not need them in your new place), and if you try to sell them you will suffer a tremendous loss. New appliances depreciate terrifically the minute they are removed from the store and become "used appliances," so get in on the other end and let this rapid depreciation work for you instead of against you. With a bit of perseverance, you can ferret out marvelous buys on all major appliances, which, should you have to, you can sell for almost what you paid for them, a year later. Newspaper classified columns and appliance dealers are the places to start your search. You usually can get better deals from private individuals—but most appliance dealers have "trade-ins" which they have rebuilt and will guarantee, so try both.

You can also get extremely good buys on secondhand washing machines. We still have the washing machine we bought three years ago from the used collection of a reputable dealer. It was five years old at the time, a well-known brand, recommended highly by *Consumers Reports*. Except for some new gadgets, the model had not changed much in the meantime. It seemed to be in good condition, inside and out (the outside is quite important for resale), and the dealer gave us a short-term guarantee. We paid $40.00 for this machine. It has never needed any repairs. It gets clothes beautifully clean and, last year when we moved, two of our friends offered to buy it from us for just what we paid for it (we were, however, able to take it with us). A very good testimonial, I feel, for a used washing machine.

A light cheery paint and a quaint print curtain may be all the decorating that is called for, indeed, possible in a small kitchen. Your personal touches might include gay dish towels, quaint cannisters, a colorful string of red Bermuda onions hanging on the wall and used from there, a group of prints or drawings, or interesting trays or plates mounted on the walls. The latter are easily mounted by hanging a coat hanger which has been bent like an upside down "v" with its ends turned up, on the wall and resting the plate or tray in the turned up ends. Sometimes apartments in old houses have large kitchens which serve as the dining area. In this case the furniture mentioned for a dining room would do well. An extra piece of furniture for this kind of kitchen or anywhere in your apartment for that matter, is a little old-fashioned school desk; these with their tops, which are often lovely wood, refinished, and their curlicue iron legs painted, are charming as little desks. In the kitchen they can hold cookbooks and note paper and elsewhere they make wonderful telephone stands. They are quite inexpensive in antique shops.

The Bathroom

Apartment bathrooms, too, are fairly well equipped. You certainly will not have to worry about your own appliances here. In choosing a color scheme it can be either pastel and pretty or bold (white with bright accents) and dramatic. The curtains (window and shower), towels, bath mats, and hamper are the major accents. Bathroom curtains can be a pretty print (if you use cotton, have it fairly heavy as the steam will wrinkle percale or glazed-type cottons—denim is wonderful) or an unobtrusive rubber or plastic if the window is on the bathtub wall. Shutters are pretty in the bathroom, too.

I have had the best luck in buying shower curtains, again in the "five-and-ten-cent" store. Instead of paying $5.00 to $10.00 for them, you pay $1.00 to $2.00 and they are in plain pretty colors instead of the typical garish prints.

Hampers are another thing which seem to inspire the most dreadful designs. I looked all over New York trying to find a decent one. I finally settled on one with a good shape but particularly ghastly "art work" which I covered with a plastic adhesive paper in a small print. This I've found to be very satisfactory. The adhesive papers hold up well in a bathroom and come in a good variety of nice little prints, checks, stripes, and plain colors. Best of all, you can change the look of your hamper quickly and inexpensively with a fresh "coat" at any time. For one apartment I found a rose and white candy-striped adhesive paper for the hamper and by great coincidence the same stripe in a cotton fabric for the bathroom curtains. There are large covered baskets, square or shaped rather like a snake charmer's which make delightful hampers, too. These should be lined with plastic or something similar so as not to snag your clothes.

Bath towels and bath mats are usually eulogized with the adjectives dense, luxurious, and thick. But I prefer the light-to-medium weight ones as they dry faster. I hate soggy towels and the really thick ones take for ever to dry. The same is true of bath mats. My favorite bath mat is a fairly heavy hand towel. This can be washed easily, replaced often, and in general, is quite satisfactory.

A pretty accent for a bathroom—a simple one, but one which I have had admired and copied over and over again—is the use of large glass apothecary jars (either unusual antique ones, or pretty new ones bought for next to nothing in the "five-and-ten") filled with colored bath articles. I have three along the top of the toilet, the center one, a large one, is filled with different colored bars of soap, and the two flanking ones hold bubble bath and bath salts.

Other decorative accents for your bathroom are plants (many plants thrive in the humid atmosphere of a bathroom; a hanging one in the window is particularly nice), Victorian hooks or brackets mounted on the wall and used as guest towel racks, a candle or kerosene lantern such as an old carriage lamp also mounted on the wall and lit for special occasions.

The Bedroom

BEDS

By far the most important item in a bedroom is, naturally, the bed. By this I do not mean the frame (the head and foot boards)—these are merely decoration which can be added later—but the mattress and springs. These should be your first major investment; no compromises should be made, nor expenses spared by getting a "bargain." "Bargain mattresses" are often the epitome of advertising's misrepresentations, so be sure of what you are getting. The "best" are seldom reduced. A good mattress is essential to your health and well-being and if cared for properly (turned often in the beginning for one thing), will last a long time, so it is important to have a really good one from the start.

A wise thing to do is buy only your mattress and springs at first. Mount these on little legs, which are especially made for this purpose and you have a comfortable bed.

The head and foot board can be added later, when you have the money and are sure of what you want. Antique shops and auctions offer a large variety of bedsteads at a reasonable price, so you might be looking at some of these for ideas. Our pride and joy is a spool bed which my mother got for me at an auction when I was a little girl. She refinished it and it is one of the most handsome beds I've seen.

One thing about spool beds, they usually come in either single or three-quarter size. Three-quarter size is only about three inches narrower than a double bed, but it should have its own size mattress and springs. Almost every manufacturer makes these and your furniture dealer can order them for you.

Brass or metal beds are also available quite inexpensively at antique shops and with certain decors are delightful. Or you can make elegant headboards from old iron gates. We have friends with such a headboard which is truly handsome. They retrieved it from an old house which was being torn down.

While we are talking about beds, I'd like to mention briefly bed linen. In spite of the fantastic amounts claimed to be needed by bride's magazines, etc., I found six sheets and six pillow cases to be plenty for a double bed and a couch (or something for guests). This allows two for each plus two extra.

CHESTS OF DRAWERS

Chests of drawers are probably the next thing you will want for your bedroom. Ultimately, of course, you will want two, but in the meantime you can share one, or use one chest of drawers and a blanket chest.

Aside from the smallish pine or poplar "cottage furniture" chests—which are versatile and can often be found at antique dealers and auctions—good chests, both antique and new, are generally rather expensive. Inexpensive ones are usually poorly made and not worth bothering with. Nowhere does poor workmanship show up as blatantly as in a chest of drawers. This poor quality is quite easily detected—I talk about this in the chapter on Buying New Furniture. So, it would be well to use your ingenuity with a discarded chest or get a little pine one, or a blanket chest in the beginning.

Attics and basements are regular treasure troves for old chests of drawers. Some of these are quite grotesque, but a coat of paint can do wonders for them. You might want to "antique" one or paint the bulk one color and trim it with another. You also might want to streamline it by cutting off its legs and removing the bric-a-brac that seemed to run rampant on tops of chests at the turn of the century. By removing the veneer, which covered many of these monstrosities, you can sometimes find quite presentable wood underneath which can easily be refinished.

One of our chests of drawers started life as a late Victorian chest. It had the "works"—spindly legs, veneer, bric-a-brac on the top. We found it in my husband's family's attic where it had been discarded. Bit by bit, we removed all its superfluities until it emerged, a simple, low three-drawer chestnut chest.

Occasionally you find a period piece of good design relegated to an attic. This, of course, you would not want to deal with so harshly. A good cleaning, or possibly refinishing, would be all that's in order.

MIRRORS

Mirrors for your chests can be had with a little bit of ingenuity at very little expense. The actual mirror glass itself can be cut in any size or shape at your local lumber yard, so all you have to do is find a frame. Again, we make a beeline for antique shops. They always have piles and piles of old picture frames, which are excellent for this purpose.

There are ornate gilt ones, some of which in their original condition are rather ghastly, but painted with flat white paint take on the aura of a lacy valentine and are charming. For a more rustic effect, there are simple veneered ones of last century, which, when the veneer is removed (this is easily done by soaking the frame in the bathtub over night), are usually lovely mellow pine. And then there are those lovely aristocratic hardwood ones, walnut usually, with a fine gilt liner.

All of these make charming, inexpensive mirror frames. Simply choose one, refinish it if necessary, and take it to the lumber yard and have it fitted with glass.

BEDSIDE TABLES

Bedside tables are handy for lamps, a telephone, reading and writing material, etc. Any of the things I mentioned for end tables in the living room could be well adapted for this purpose.

CURTAINS AND RUGS

Curtains and rugs for your bedroom are also mostly adaptations of those for the living room, although I'd especially advocate small cotton "throw" rugs here. These are inexpensive, attractive and easy to clean—you can wash them in the washing machine. Small braided rugs, are, of course, delightful in early American bedrooms.

As for curtains, if you want a fluffier curtain than those described for the living room, you might want to get dotted swiss, organdy or some other airy fabric, or they can be had ready-made. The ready-made ones are not necessarily expensive and when a rather standard fluffy white curtain is wanted, are quite satisfactory. Also, charming bedroom curtains can easily be made from cotton prints, mattress ticking, muslins, etc. Usually I use tape with loops, which is simply sewn across the top, or the clip-on rings, rather than pleater tape for bedroom curtains.

General

Besides specific furniture suggestions, each accommodation you live in will need some specific attention of its own. We are very aware of this having just decorated a rather ungainly Victorian apartment and I would like to pass on a few of the inexpensive touches we gave to it. They may give you ideas which you can vary or adapt to your needs.

This house, as do many of its era, has exposed radiators covered at the top with a plank which forms a window seat. Since we were running out of funds, we simply painted the radiators the same colors as the walls, instead of the ugly silver they had been. A slightly more expensive but still reasonable and very attractive way of camouflaging these radiators is to cover their fronts with punched aluminum. This comes in sheets, punched in various designs which, when covering a radiator, gives a filigree effect that in no way interferes with the heat efficiency. You can paint these the wall color or a contrasting one—black in a Spanish-flavored room would be nice.

We "carpeted" the window seats with cotton throw rugs which we bought at a "five-and-ten-cent" store and cut to fit (some we had to piece a bit), and tacked to the underpart of the seat with carpet tacks. On one seat we used the remains of an old rug pad as a pad but this is not necessary. This "carpeting" of the window seats was extremely inexpensive, particularly in comparison to the elaborate foam cushions used by many, and has proved to be very attractive and practical. The vacuum cleaner cleans them except when they are really soiled. At that point I remove the tacks and put the covers in the washing machine.

The closet floors of the apartment were in deplorable condition, splintery, uneven, and dirty. The answer—adhesive paper again. We simply covered the floors with a gay pattern and have a very attractive and easy to clean "linoleum" floor.

Another problem was the lack of a corner for our corner cupboard. With the built-in bookcases windows, etc., there literally was not a corner for it. We finally solved this by putting one of its sides against the wall, thereby having the front facing diagonally into a little section we planned to use as a dining room. But the other side (which as in the case of most antique corner cupboards, is unfinished) was facing the living room. This we covered with burlap—any fabric would do—and hung our horse brasses on it. The result is a very satisfactory room divider. This treatment could be used quite well on any large piece of furniture you wanted to use this way.

One thing we learned the hard way from this most recent move is that gloss enamel on the woodwork is a must for an old city apartment. Over the loud protests of the landlady, I insisted on flat enamel for the door, windows, etc. I much prefer dull paint and I blithely said I was willing to wash the woodwork a bit oftener to have it. But the dull paint is almost impossible to keep clean. The city soot seeps in and instead of being able to whisk it away with a cloth or vacuum cleaner as one can from a glossy surface, it smudges and grinds into the dull finish. Regular scrubbing takes care of it for a few weeks until the paint begins to peel. Then you have to begin all over again. So let me heartily recommend—almost insist on—glossy enamel for woodwork.

This is an example of decorating through experience. Experimenting is fun. Everyone has some things he must try for himself—no amount of talk will dissuade him. He won't be satisfied until he sees the results. The very best results for you are often achieved this way, but so, too, are the fiascoes. May you have many of the first and few of the last.

ELEVEN

DECORATING YOUR DINING TABLE

◻

DISHES, glasses, and flatware are often put in two categories, "everyday" and "good." This, of course, is a carry-over from the time, not too long ago, when average people did quite a bit of formal entertaining as well as "everyday" living and the two were worlds apart. But in most places this is no longer true. Today, almost all of a young couple's entertaining is of an informal nature. With the lack of domestic help, their parent's generation is getting away from formal living, also.

I have a friend who had a big wedding and got "the works": formal china, crystal stemware for every conceivable wine and beverage, sterling flatware and hollow ware. Then almost as an afterthought she got some rather nondescript dishes, glasses, and stainless steel for "everyday." Well, up until last year when she gave up in despair and used her bone china and sterling silver for a chicken barbecue, she had, in three years, used her formal table settings once. In the meantime, she and her company had used regularly, the uninteresting, hastily chosen "everydays" while the others, the carefully chosen ones, gathered dust. This doesn't quite make sense, does it?

In an age when the emphasis is on informality, where elegance is informal elegance and gracious living is informal living, doesn't it seem much more reasonable to put the main emphasis on the things which you are going to use every day? After all you have a right to enjoy them too, and you will be using the "everyday" things for most of your company anyway.

What I'm getting at is this: If having a "good" set means scrimping and having a very makeshift everyday one, I think it is far better to get one set of really elegant, informal dishes (probably pottery), and simple flatware, and glasses. Then you will enjoy them every day and they will make your informal entertaining elegant and special.

What about the few times you *would* use the formal ones? In most places I don't think there would be a time when elegant pottery with a rough linen cloth and complementary accessories would not be acceptable, indeed delightful. The one exception might be an afternoon tea.

A tea's very nature suggests more delicate things. This can be solved very nicely with an ever-growing collection (six to twelve to start) of tea cups. Assorted antique ones, which you can find relatively inexpensively at auctions and shops, are fun to collect and are charming for the purpose. Extra cups are always welcome and these cups can be used as such, if and when you decide to get a set of formal china. In this way you can collect little silver tea spoons, too, and these can always be used as "extras" later as well.

Dishes

Depending on your taste, you may want your one set of dishes to be a simple but fine china, or earthenware, in which case I would recommend white as it is so versatile. With a brilliant cloth and accessories, such dishes can be striking and dramatic, or with softer colors, they can be delicate or even dainty.

If you prefer a more rugged look, heavy pottery dishes, to be used with wooden bowls and copper and brass accessories, probably are the things for you. Again choose a neutral color. Ironstone is lovely in white, but most heavy pottery comes in earth colors—browns, mustards, beiges, some blues and greens.

Choose a pattern, which is listed as "open stock." This means that it is a continuous pattern, can be bought by the piece, and will be available in the foreseeable future, allowing you to get additional pieces as you need them, or replace those you break. Place settings for six and some serving dishes and a casserole are usually enough in the beginning, but you will probably want to add more place settings and special pieces later.

If you live near a city, you may very well be able to find a store or factory salesroom which sells "seconds." These, for some reason, often undiscernable, are less than perfect and are sold for a much reduced price. Some stores make a business of going around to various factories here and abroad gathering up such rejects. These are good buys. We got our own dishes from such a place in New York called The Pottery Barn, which specializes in European pottery and stainless steel. It is on 10th Avenue for those of you who are near New York City.

Be sure the dishes you get from such a place are "open stock," if not at the "second store" at a regular store.

Besides place settings, which usually include dinner plates, salad plates, bread and butter plates, and cups and saucers, you will need some extra pieces such as salad bowls, platters, sugar and creamers, salt and pepper shakers, etc. The choice of these is dictated by your choice of dishes. If your dishes are rustic, polished wooden bowls, brass, copper, and pewter would all be in keeping with them. If your dishes are more dainty, crystal, silver, pewter, and less rustic woods would be lovely.

Also I think a set of small bowls which complement your china are indispensable. They have numerous functions; salads, desserts, grapefruit, and soups, to name a few.

Flatware

Barring a trip through a garbage grinder, or something equally disastrous, any flatware is practically indestructible, so from a practical standpoint, there is no reason why you can't use anything your taste, your choice of dishes and your budget dictates, for literally every day.

Flatware should, of course, be of a similar character as

that of your dishes. If your dishes are delicate, a dainty silver pattern would be fine, but if your dishes are more rugged, a simple silver or stainless steel pattern would be better.

Stainless steel, which used to be primarily a kitchen metal, has come into its own with elegant patterns which can be used with all but the most formal china, and handsomely, for all but the most formal occasions.

If, however, you want sterling (I shy away from silver plate, because it does not fit in with my premise of getting the best of what you are buying: Plate is a weak substitute for silver; the choice of patterns is limited and most important of all, plate does wear off) and your budget can stand it, don't hesitate to buy silver as your one and only, and use it with pleasure all the time. I have a friend who does this and claims that with constant use, silver seldom needs to be polished, except to remove egg and mayonnaise tarnish, and that the patina of the silver is actually improved. Whatever did it, her silver does have a lovely mellow look.

Again choose a pattern which is in keeping not only with the dishes you want now, but those you anticipate having in the future. A fairly simple one is usually the best choice. Obviously, you won't need any more place settings of silver than dishes, so six place settings and a few serving spoons is a good amount to start with here, too.

Glasses

Glasses present a slightly different problem as there are traditionally many different sizes and shapes for different beverages and occasions. These are: tumblers, water goblets, fruit juice glasses, sherbets, cocktail glasses, highball glasses, old-fashioned glasses, table wine glasses (red and white), sherry glasses, liqueur glasses, and champagne glasses.

Undoubtedly, with a small budget, you will not be serving all the beverages indicated by this array. But you should have proper glasses for those you do serve. Beverages, alcoholic and other, are steeped in tradition and an aura of elegance which demands the proper equipment to have them truly festive. There is, however, enough similarity in many of these glasses for you to double up their functions and still win the approval of Amy Vanderbilt.

Unless your dishes are rather dainty and you have a craving for water goblets, large eight-ounce tumblers can suffice for water glasses, highball glasses, and any other long drink glasses. Simple fruit juice glasses can double as old-fashioned glasses. Sherbets and champagnes can be one and the same. Cocktail glasses can be used for sherry, and a clear all-purpose wine glass can be used for either red or white wine. Brandy and liqueur glasses though, are brandy and liqueur glasses and "ever more shall be so."

This still leaves you with six sets of glasses, so in the beginning buy only the ones you will be using. Often tumblers, and juice glasses (you can get away with serving cocktails in a juice old-fashioned glass) will be enough at first.

Choose glasses which go well with your dishes. Remember that uncolored glass is traditionally used for wines and liqueurs, so their colors will be clearly visible.

Clarity and a clear ring are the marks of fine crystal. Hold a piece of glass up to the light and you will be able to see its flaws or beauty.

Glasses, too, often can be found at stores handling seconds. Again be sure of their continued availability somewhere.

Table Linens

Except in the case of a family heirloom, table linens should be considered last, and then chosen for their ability to accent and complement your dishes.

For regular use, I am a strong believer in place mats; they are attractive and easy to care for. My favorites are the woven straw or rush ones. These come in a wide assortment of rich, glowing colors, as well as subtle neutrals, and they wipe clean with a damp sponge. They can be bought in any number. Six is a good number, but you can have some sets of different amounts. It is surprising how the whole atmosphere of your dishes can change with their background. So *do* have several different harmonizing colors for different effects. These can also be used as the mats for flower arrangements.

Terry cloth guest towels, of all things, make practical and pretty place mats. These are inexpensive, are just the right size, launder easily with no ironing, and come in lovely colors. For a complete effect, I have bought striped linen dish towels in a matching color, cut them in half, fringed the ends and had gay "matching" napkins.

For the special occasions when you want to use a table-cloth, don't feel that the old standby, a white linen one, is the only answer. White is nice, just as any other "color" is nice when it shows off the table's furnishings to the best advantage, but that is all. No longer is white "necessary" for a formal dinner.

Since it is so basic, I would suggest having one white or off-white tablecloth for the occasions when no other cloth you have seems to go with your mood or flowers. Then have pastel, or dramatic colored linen cloths which complement your dishes and your entertaining.

Simple Belgian linen cloths can be bought very inexpensively in all sizes. Watch the city newspapers for department store ads. How many, and the sizes of tablecloths will depend on you, your table, your entertaining, and your ideas for different color schemes.

Napkins are a touchy subject. Not too many years ago, nobody would have thought of using anything but linen napkins. Today, in spite of the hesitant acceptance and general use of paper napkins, linen napkins still are preferable. If you balk at using linen napkins, with napkin rings (some of these are so attractive, they might be an incentive) for you and your husband when you are alone, use paper ones—even use paper ones for your really casual entertaining, but when you are having any kind of special affair, do use linen napkins.

If you want to invest in just a few napkins, white are the ones to buy. Plain white linen napkins will go with any color scheme or decor, so have at least a dozen of these. But if you can, buy several sets of napkins; ones which contrast or blend with your tablecloth and accessories are lovely. Also, you can make charming inexpensive napkins by fringing squares of pretty print cotton.

The Bride of a Large Wedding.—Modern efficiency and organization have the bride of a large wedding listing her china, silver, linen, and crystal patterns at various prominent stores, often insuring herself of almost all the equipment needed for the two broad categories, "good" and "everyday." Be it sufficient to say, if at no hardship to you or your family, you can have and want all this equipment, fine! But my advice to you is again, buy only what you like and the best of what you are buying for both special occasions and everyday use; don't sacrifice one for the other. Consult an etiquette book to find out what is "correct" for which formal occasions. Formal entertaining has certain protocol. That is what makes it formal after all, and, if you are going in for it, this should be observed lest you emerge with an ostentatious display instead of formal perfection.

With that bit of advice I turn you, who are planning on having the "works," over to the etiquette books.

APPENDIX

□

ITALY

Italian Renaissance—1453 to 1550

ATMOSPHERE

Rich, elegant, royal, classical forms used. Revival of Egyptian, Greek, Roman, and Byzantine arts.

FURNITURE CHARACTERISTICS AND WOODS

Massive, straight-lined, and simple but with elaborate carvings. Gesso work, relief molded from chalk and white lead, polychrome inlay, and metal ornaments. Motifs: acanthus leaves, rosettes, cupids, caryatids, and festoons. X chair introduced. Stamped leather used. Feet: rectangular floor runner or block or lion. The cassone (an elaborately carved chest) particularly significant. Wood: oak and walnut.

ACCESSORIES

Venetian glass, Florentine cut velvets, murals and tapestries, marble, tile, and oak floors, brass and iron candelabra, pottery vases, Della Robbia plaques, mirrors introduced, small Oriental rugs.

COLORS AND FABRICS

Brilliant red, green, purple, yellow, blue, gold. Cut velvets, brocades, damasks with large bold patterns and fringes.

Italy was dictating the European styles at this time. This is one of the richest periods in the history of art. Many of the greatest artists worked in it.

Baroque and Rococo—1550 to 1750

ATMOSPHERE

Italian Renaissance exaggerated—bright, brittle, cloying, theatrical.

FURNITURE CHARACTERISTICS AND WOODS

Florid and meaningless ornaments, overdecorated. Woods: oak and walnut.

ACCESSORIES

All the Renaissance accessories exaggerated. Marble floors, walls either painted or covered with a marbleized paper called "domino."

COLORS AND FABRICS

Brilliant colors or delicate ones of white, ivory, and gray with gold.

REMARKS

This period saw the decline of Italian creativity. France was to take over as European style leader.

SPAIN

Spanish Renaissance—1500 to 1700

ATMOSPHERE

Strong contrasts, airiness. The Moorish influence is predominant. A love of splendor, bright colors, and geometric designs is the key. Bold, informal, but dignified.

FURNITURE CHARACTERISTICS AND WOODS

Large and geometric. Chairs with rush, leather, or wood seats; also X chairs; legs straight or splayed, spiraled and heavily turned, often braced with iron; bun and Spanish scroll feet. Tooled leather significant, lacquer work and inlay. Motifs: geometrical designs and acanthus leaf. Much iron used in supports and grilles. Large round ornamental brass and iron nailheads, locks, and key plates. Carved finials— sometimes brass—often adorn chair backs. Woods: oak, walnut, and some chestnut and red pine.

ACCESSORIES

Brick or tile floors in red, black, and white; much ironwork; candelabra, stands, etc. Decorative tiles, floor cushions. Oriental and Spanish Alpajura rugs. Tapestries and Oriental rugs used as wall hangings.

COLORS AND FABRICS

High color against white or neutral grounds. Reds, blacks, blues, greens, oranges, and yellows. Fringed velvet, damasks, tooled leather, crewel embroideries, heraldic designs.

REMARKS

The most prosperous and brilliant period in Spanish history and in her arts.

NETHERLANDS AND BELGIUM

Dutch and Flemish Renaissance—1500 to 1650

Stolid, heavy, frequently clumsy. The sixteenth-century style was mainly Spanish Provincial.

FURNITURE CHARACTERISTICS AND WOODS

The most significant feature of this style was the cabriole leg, which was of Chinese origin and was later adopted by the English for their Queen Anne style. Indeed, many features of the English styles were inspired by this period: the Flemish scroll and the spiral turnings were features of the Charles II period. Geometrical-patterned moldings applied to flat surfaces are seen in the English Jacobean and in Early American pieces—low, flat, decorative underbracings, shaped-apron tables, and the bun feet were borrowed by the William and Mary period. Other features were straight-backed chairs, some with cane insets in the backs and seats. Much carving, inlay, and marquetry. Motifs: shell, acanthus leaf, lion heads, and foliage. Ornamented stretchers, turned and vase-shaped legs. Woods: oak and walnut.

ACCESSORIES

Iron candelabra, paintings, Oriental rugs, tapestries—the first significant tapestries were made in Flanders as early as 1100. Chinese bric-a-brac, vases, dragons, and porcelain.

COLORS AND FABRICS

Red, green, yellow. Tapestries and velvets, ornamental leathers.

REMARKS

The significance of this style is its inspiration for so much English furniture and in turn Early American. Up until 1581, Holland and Flanders were one country ruled by Spain. So naturally their styles were the same, with a definite Spanish influence. But in 1581 Holland broke away and developed a style of her own, influenced by her dealings with the Orient.

CENTRAL EUROPE

(From the Balkan States northward through Czechoslovakia, Austria, Switzerland, and Scandinavia)

Peasant Furniture of Europe—Up to Industrial Revolution—about 1850

ATMOSPHERE

Extremely rustic, utilitarian, homey, cozy.

FURNITURE CHARACTERISTICS AND WOODS

Crude forms, gross and clumsy. Painted designs, often of human figures and floral and animal forms. Naïve carvings mostly geometric—abstract designs showed regional stylization. All these elements combined to make for a charming thoroughly sincere atmosphere indicating the conscientiousness and love felt by the peasant workman for his craft. Simple furniture such as chairs, stools, tables, beds—sometimes enclosed—chests, wardrobes, cupboards, plate shelves, and dressers were the usual pieces. Woods: since furniture was usually painted, no particular effect was wanted from the woods themselves. Therefore what was easiest to work for a specific piece and what was on hand were the deciding factors. Often several different woods were used in one piece of furniture.

ACCESSORIES

Embroideries, tiles, pottery, clocks, pewter utensils and tableware, tin and wooden molds, brass and iron utensils, many of these fashioned by the ingenious peasants themselves. Handwoven and braided rugs.

COLORS AND FABRICS

Vivid and primary colors. Homespun fabrics.

REMARKS

These were true peasant styles. None of these countries had produced original court or formal styles so their peasant styles were their contribution to the arts. Peasant styles were, of course, produced in Italy, Spain, France, and England, but they were so strongly influenced by court styles as to be just a variation of these and the provincial interpretations.

GERMANY

Biedermeier—1800 to 1850

Plump, straightforward, provincial, naïve, quaint, solid, homely, droll.

The inspiration for this style was French Empire and German painted peasant work. Since this was an imitative style the furniture varied in quality of design and structure, but in general it was quaint, sturdy, rectangular, and often awkward, although many small delicate pieces with rather clumsy curves were produced. The motifs were similar to Empire, although the emphasis was on flora and fauna rather than on the imperialistic symbols, and fashioned of brass or painted on furniture with black enamel. Much enamel was used in black, brown, and colors—also gilt. Little carving was used but surfaces were enriched with simple marquetry patterns and borders, and brass ornaments of Greek inspiration. Diamond-shaped lines and moldings were much used. Woods: usually native light-colored fruitwoods, and maple, birch and elm, which offered a strong contrast to the dark lacquer used.

Those of the Empire period.

Stark contrast—black or deep-toned upholstery with light-colored woods and white or light colors with black lacquered pieces. Again the fabrics were mainly those of the French Empire, with some more homey additions.

REMARKS

The name Biedermeier was borrowed from a humorous self-satisfied, opinionated cartoon character named Papa Biedermeier which appeared in a German illustrated paper of the time. The style has been enjoying some recent popularity in reproductions as well as originals. Aside from this unique development in German furniture, its trends were those of other European countries considered in this outline. The bentwood chairs which are so popular today, though not considered Biedermeier, are of the same time. They were created by Michael Thonet, who, in 1836, discovered a way of bending wood by heating it in steam.

FRANCE

French Renaissance—1515 to 1643

ATMOSPHERE

Grand, impressive, formal, Italian influence predominates except for the Provincial French, which displayed more native characteristics.

FURNITURE CHARACTERISTICS AND WOODS

Adaptations of Italian furniture with some Gothic influence. Carvings of Italian motifs with classic grace and columns. Motifs: carved acanthus pattern, also fleur-de-lis, human forms and heads, mythological creatures. Woods: oak and walnut.

ACCESSORIES

Parquet floors, walls painted or covered with Italian marbleized paper, Oriental rugs, wood paneling, brass and iron candelabra, clocks, vases, statuettes.

COLORS AND FABRICS

Rich reds, blues, greens, yellows, and purples. Corded and tasseled velvets, brocades, tapestries, often with large patterns.

REMARKS

This, too, was a very prosperous period with a great advancement in the arts. The famous châteaux at Blois, Chambord and Fontainebleau were built.

Louis XIV—1643 to 1715

ATMOSPHERE

Known as the regal age or golden age. Splendor and magnificence. The most magnificent period in history. Primarily Renaissance influence. Baroque.

FURNITURE CHARACTERISTICS AND WOODS

Massive forms, rectilinear and classic—broken by carving and baroque embellishment. Some curves. Motifs: Louis XIV sunburst particularly distinctive. Also acanthus leaves, shell and floral forms and classic motifs. Heavily carved straight legs with X-shaped stretchers. Some pedestals. High backed chairs. Caning came in in 1690. Marble table tops, much inlay, marquetry, and lacquer. Woods: oak, walnut, ebony, and chestnut. Many rare colored woods and tortoise shell for marquetry and inlay.

ACCESSORIES

Much gilt, large gilt-framed mirrors, some black and white marble floors but usually parquet. French and Oriental carpets, tapestries, wall sconces, Chinese porcelain, Boule work, Chinese wallpaper, profuse use of valances, crystal chandeliers, metal mounts of ormolu.

COLORS AND FABRICS

Rich, intense. Gilt, crimson, green, blue, yellow. Fabrics rich and gorgeous: damasks, silks, brocades in large, formal patterns, often worked with gold thread.

REMARKS

Although inspired by Italy, the first purely native style. Boule, the greatest artist with inlay, worked at this time. Gobelin's tapestry factory influential. The palace at Versailles, which was originally a hunting lodge, was turned into the most magnificent palace in the world.

French Regency—1715 to 1743

ATMOSPHERE

A transitional period between the formal style of Louis XIV and the less formal style of Louis XV. Smaller scale rooms and furniture than those of Louis XIV.

FURNITURE CHARACTERISTICS AND WOODS

Louis XIV forms mostly retained with a few introductions, such as slightly curving legs replacing straight ones. Cabriole legs with scroll feet. In general the effect was a lighter and more curvaceous one than Louis XIV. Motifs: foliage and ribbon ornament and beginning of rococo figures. Marble tops on commodes, tables, and dressers. Inlay still popular. Woods: mahogany, rosewood, and walnut.

ACCESSORIES

Elaborate mirrors, valances everywhere, crystal chandeliers, Chinese and Oriental rugs, parquet floors, marble fireplaces, wall panels of stucco relief, carvings.

COLORS AND FABRICS

Louis XIV's colors were softened to rose, silver, powder blue, pearl gray, light green with silver and gold. Fabrics: silks, satins, brocades, and taffetas.

REMARKS

The French government was practically bankrupt from the opulence of the preceding period. There are two famous artists of the period—Antoine Watteau, the painter, and Giles Oppenort, the designer.

Louis XV—1723 to 1774

ATMOSPHERE

Feminine, intimate, sentimental. "France became one huge boudoir." Chinese influence. Rococo—named for the use of shell and rock motifs.

FURNITURE CHARACTERISTICS AND WOODS

Small, dainty, graceful. Free-flowing curves everywhere— particularly S curves. Seating pieces either had upholstery (little pads on arms were particularly distinctive) or were caned. Often gilded caning. Embellishments were light and gay. Motifs: dolphin heads, wreaths, flowers, ribbons, shells, cupids, and figures abounded. Chinese lacquer. A jazzed-up version of England's Queen Anne style. Woods: oak, mahogany, walnut, beech, ebony, maple, rosewood, tulipwood, labernum, holly, and pear.

ACCESSORIES

Metalwork, mirrors, porcelain collections, Chinese art objects, parquet floors, stucco carvings in relief and paintings in panels, silver candlesticks, Chinese wallpapers, ormolu. Aubusson, Chinese, and Oriental rugs in delicate colors.

COLORS AND FABRICS

Rose, dove gray, silver, gold, white, powder blue, light green. Fabrics: brocades, silks, satins, damasks, printed cottons, toiles de Jouy (introduced by Oberkampf in 1759), taffetas, needlepoint, velvets.

REMARKS

Madame de Pompadour and Madame du Barry influenced the period. The most widely reproduced of the French periods. Most of the French Provincial so popular today was the provincial French—a simplified version of court styles—of Louis XV.

Louis XVI—1774 to 1793

ATMOSPHERE

Elegant, refined, classic. Classic influence. Neo-Grecque.

FURNITURE CHARACTERISTICS AND WOODS

Small, natural, simple rectangular forms. Straight lines; legs were straight and tapered (some had square blocks with rosette at the top), decorated with fluting, reeding, or some carving. Motifs: urns, lyres, oak and acanthus leaves, torches, garlands of flowers; some inlay in classic designs. Marble tops still used. Ivory or ivory-paneled miniatures. Subdued lacquer. Woods: mahogany, beech, walnut, rosewood, satinwood.

ACCESSORIES

Small pieces with classic motifs: many exquisite knickknacks; terra-cotta nymphs and satyrs by artist Cloden; urns, statuettes; oil lamps introduced, metalwork, ormolu mounts, parquet floors. French Savonnerie, Aubusson and Oriental rugs.

COLORS AND FABRICS

Colors were lighter at first and stronger later. White, gold, gray, greens, and blues, pinks, fawns, and other muted shades replaced by crimsons, greens, blues, and yellows. Fabrics: toiles de Jouy were very popular, cottons, Lyons silks, taffetas, and satins. Striped and floral designs; feather motif also popular.

REMARKS

Marie Antoinette was the main influence here. Today this style is second only to Louis XV in popularity.

French Provincial—1643 to 1793

ATMOSPHERE

French Provincial is, as the name implies, the provinces' interpretation of Parisian style. It varied slightly from king to king. Louis XV's examples were most popular. It was usually employed by the merchants in their country châteaux and the general effect was rustic. Norman architecture and beamed ceilings prevailed.

FURNITURE CHARACTERISTICS AND WOODS

Proportions were medium to heavy; lines were bold—straight or modified curves. Cabriole legs were used extensively. Local interpretations of the Louis' styles—motifs were less elaborate.

Huge armoires were particularly popular. Much upholstery used. Most pieces were straightforward and functional. Woods: oak, pine, beech, chestnut, fruitwoods.

ACCESSORIES

Pottery, brass, pewter, wrought iron. Small, wooden-framed mirrors and prints. Brick fireplaces, braided rugs.

COLORS AND FABRICS

Reds, blues, browns, and warm greens, yellows, tans, and creams. Also softer tones—roses, blues, and greens. Fabrics ranged from fine silks and toiles de Jouy to homespun woolens and checked ginghams. Ginghams, chintzes, quilted fabrics and toiles de Jouy predominated.

REMARKS

This style represents local and economic interpretations of court styles. Sometimes the interpretations were extremely crude (when the peasants copied it) and sometimes more refined (when commissioned by the wealthy merchants). There was little attempt to copy the late Louis XVI styles, however.

Directoire—1795 to 1799

ATMOSPHERE

This style, named for the Directory of Five which governed during these years, marked a decided change in furnishings from those before the Revolution. All monarchistic symbols were eliminated and replaced by classic Greek and Roman ones. This style was a combination of austere simplicity and charm.

FURNITURE CHARACTERISTICS AND WOODS

Rectangular lines combined with Greek curve and scroll. Front chair legs were straight while back ones flared out. Painted ornamentation replaced carving and inlay. Motifs:

classic forms, such as torches, swans, urns, hunters and animals, lyres, swags, etc. The tables were significant, particularly those with a circular top resting on three C-shaped legs adorned with griffins' or rams' heads and feet. Woods: mahogany predominated, considerable veneering used, also rosewood and chestnut.

ACCESSORIES

Brass and bronze lion-headed drawer pulls, bronze and marble statuettes, urns, clocks, pier glasses, paintings by artist Jacques Louis David, parquet floors—although occasionally marble; French woven carpets with classical designs.

COLORS AND FABRICS

Deep yellows, Pompeian reds and greens, brown, blue, purple, black. Richly colored silks, satins and moirés, having formal classic motifs or very fine stripes. Toiles de Jouy with landscapes or motif designs.

REMARKS

The Directoire style was the forerunner of the Empire style and because of the short period of time involved, it is hard to tell where one stops and the other begins.

French Empire—1799 to 1815

ATMOSPHERE

Formal, ornate, cold, ponderous, symmetrical, masculine. Greek and Roman influence, also Egyptian from Napoleon's Egyptian campaign.

FURNITURE CHARACTERISTICS AND WOODS

Napoleonic conceit dominated. The letter N was found everywhere in the motifs, as were symbols of conquest such as crossed swords, fasces, urns, bees, pineapples, winged victories. Also sphinx, swans, griffins and other animals. There were many backless, rolled armed couches, sofas, and daybeds. Painting and metal mounts instead of carving. Woods: mahogany predominated, considerable veneering used, also rosewood and chestnut.

ACCESSORIES

Much gold, silver, and brass. Ormolu used everywhere; porcelain urns, vases, and statuettes, often on pedestals; blue and white Wedgwood plaques; accessories with Egyptian themes. Parquet floors; classic design carpets.

COLORS AND FABRICS

Bold contrasting colors such as wine reds, bright blues, purples, greens, and browns, against gray, green, and cherry-pink walls. Much gold used for trimmings. Rich silks, satins, and velvets, with spot pattern design or stripes. Toiles de Jouy.

REMARKS

Although this style officially ended with Napoleon in 1815, it continued in variations until about 1830. Jacques Louis David, the painter, commissioned by Napoleon as art director, was "the man of the hour."

Post-Empire—1815 to 1900

An unsettled atmosphere prevailed both in politics and the arts. Up until about 1830, the furniture characteristics were those of Napoleon's Empire period. Then in 1830, when Louis Philippe began his reign, there was an exaggerated revival of the French Louis XV style. This complete and wholehearted switch from the rather somber style of the Empire period can be attributed to two things. First, the people were tired of war and all its memories symbolized in the nationalistic style of Napoleon and thus were all too glad to revert to a style of gayer times. And, second, the machine age created a class of *nouveau riche* who embraced this style for all its opulence and embellished it even further. The culmination of this passion for exaggerated ornamentation was the *Art Nouveau* style, which had its crowning glory in the Paris Exposition of 1900. The motifs of the *Art Nouveau* were tree roots, trunks, and branches, waves, and irises—all twisted into grotesque shapes and patterns. The French revival of the Louis XV style with its dark woods—mahogany, rosewood, and walnut predominating—elaborate veneers, fussy accessories, and plush velours and silks set the stage for the major trends in the Victorian style of England and America.

ENGLAND

Tudor—1500 to 1558

ATMOSPHERE

Masculine, dignified, somber. Primarily Gothic influence. (Gothic, the last period of the Middle Ages, held sway in England, France, Italy, Spain, and Germany from about 1100 until 1500. It was an ecclesiastical style.) The architecture was quite significant—half-timbered exteriors and magnificent paneled interiors, exposed beams, bay windows. The pointed Tudor arch seen everywhere. Windows with leaded panes.

FURNITURE CHARACTERISTICS AND WOODS

Massive, straight-lined—made for service rather than comfort. Crudely carved patterns, usually raised. Motifs: Tudor rose, Tudor arch, human heads, linenfold, and grapevine. Chairs and tables were straight and rectangular with heavy underbracings—sometimes a boxlike effect. Little upholstery. Wood: oak.

ACCESSORIES

Tapestries, heraldic shields, armor, wooden plates, iron candelabra, paintings, Oriental rugs. The tremendous Tudor arched fireplace dominated the room.

COLORS AND FABRICS

Rich deep reds, greens, yellows, blues. Large bold patterns, crewel embroideries, hand-blocked linens, velvets, damasks.

REMARKS

The Renaissance came later to England than to many European countries. Therefore England was to turn to Italy for much of her inspiration.

Elizabethan—1558 to 1603

ATMOSPHERE

Rich, stately, still some Gothic but Renaissance beginning to predominate—the architecture still Tudor but more refined, with interiors having beamed vertical skeletons.

FURNITURE CHARACTERISTICS AND WOODS

Still heavy and straight but with the straight lines beginning to yield slightly. Heavy bulbous turnings (resembling a large melon) sometimes tipped by a crude Ionic cap. Crude, raised carvings of interlaced strapwork. Motifs: human figures, acanthus leaves and heraldic designs. Court cupboards became popular. Little upholstery. Wood: oak.

ACCESSORIES

Chinese pottery, cloisonné vases, Oriental rugs, pewter pieces, paintings, mirrors in heavy oak frames, iron candelabra, tapestries.

COLORS AND FABRICS

Rich reds, greens, yellows, and blues. Beautiful fabrics a feature—hand-blocked linens, crewel embroideries, silk damasks, India prints, tapestries, velvets, and leathers.

REMARKS

Though Queen Elizabeth was the last Tudor monarch, her reign was so important to the development of the arts as to be treated as a separate period. This is the best style for an English manor house effect.

Early Jacobean—1603 to 1649

ATMOSPHERE

Sturdy, subdued—a much more subdued style than the Elizabethan. Still a mixture of Gothic and Renaissance, but Renaissance the stronger. Flemish Renaissance influence seen.

FURNITURE CHARACTERISTICS AND WOODS

Lighter in weight and less carving than in the Elizabethan period. Motifs: acorns, heads, geometrical moldings—diamonds and lozenges. Legs were straight or turned, often with bun feet. Still little upholstery. Wood: oak.

ACCESSORIES

Chinese vases, jugs, iron candlesticks, iron candelabra, tapestries, paintings, small mirrors in oak frames, Oriental rugs.

COLORS AND FABRICS

Greens, browns, reds and yellows. Bold patterned crewel embroideries, painted linens, tapestries, leathers, velvets.

REMARKS

This style was the source of much Early American furniture, since the settlers of America brought much of it with them. It has been reproduced mainly for dining-room use. Inigo Jones, the well known architect, worked at this time.

Cromwellian—1649 to 1660

ATMOSPHERE

Extremely severe; any form of show was frowned upon by the Puritan champion of the common people, Oliver Cromwell.

FURNITURE CHARACTERISTICS AND WOODS

This style is one of the plainest of all furniture styles—the only ornamentation was some paneling. However, construction improved. Straight or turned legs with block or bun feet. Gateleg tables and Welsh dressers made their appearance. Wood: oak.

ACCESSORIES

Pewter bowls and pitchers, Bible boxes, iron candlesticks, paintings, tapestries, braided rugs.

Drab greens, grays, and browns. Monk's cloth and other rough fabrics, leather.

REMARKS

This style, too, was brought to America by the Colonists and was copied in the New World.

Restoration (Late Jacobean, Carolean, or Charles II)—1660 to 1688

ATMOSPHERE

Rich—royalty had been restored to power and there was as complete a switch as imaginable from the severity of the previous period. Cromwell had disposed of the fine furnishings of the palaces, and Charles II refurnished them with the Flemish styles he had seen while in exile.

FURNITURE CHARACTERISTICS AND WOODS

An elaborate style of medium weight. Some curves were added, as was upholstery on most chairs. Legs were straight, spiraled, or turned; underbracings low and often carved; tops spiraled—elaborate carvings. Motifs: royal crown, Flemish scroll and mitered moldings. Tea, coffee and cocoa came to England, as did cards—thus the birth of "card" or "coffee" tables. Some cane insets. Woods: oak; walnut introduced.

ACCESSORIES

Brass candlesticks, chandeliers, plates, Chinese jars and vases, paintings, mirrors in carved frames, Oriental rugs.

COLORS AND FABRICS

Rich reds, blues, greens, and yellows. Rich velvets, damasks, silks, tapestries, brocades, crewel embroideries—many with large floral, foliage, and bird designs.

This period boasted two extremely famous craftsmen—Sir Christopher Wren, the architect, and Grinling Gibbons, a famous woodcarver and sculptor.

William and Mary—1688 to 1702

ATMOSPHERE

Domestic, homey, livable; a decided Dutch influence brought in, of course, by the Dutch William of Orange. Since the Dutch style included Spanish and Oriental influences, these two elements were seen also.

FURNITURE CHARACTERISTICS AND WOODS

Medium weight, comfort considered. Wing chairs and highboys introduced. Chairs and tables now had curved and crossed underbracings and legs with trumpet shaping and inverted cup tops. Veneering, marquetry, and shaped aprons. Lacquer work came in. Motifs: floral, acanthus leaf, cockle shell, seaweed, and typical Chinese designs. Caning. Woods: walnut, but oak still used.

ACCESSORIES

Chinese porcelains, brass hardware often with teardrop designs, brass chandeliers, paintings, clocks (grandfather clocks introduced), Oriental rugs.

COLORS AND FABRICS

Reds, greens, blues, yellows, and gold—sometimes showing a feminine softness. Fine needlepoints (Queen Mary excelled in this and lent inspiration), velvets, Dutch prints, hand-blocked linens, chintz—free foliage design.

REMARKS

For the first time we see rooms as we know them today. Before this time, home comforts belonged only to the very wealthy; now they were enjoyed by the middle class. This style has been widely reproduced.

Queen Anne—1702 to 1714

ATMOSPHERE

Graceful and beautiful—a refinement of William and Mary style. Simple elegance. Beauty of wood and grace rather than ornamentation are the ingredients of this period.

FURNITURE CHARACTERISTICS AND WOODS

Graceful, comfortable furniture, curved line dominated; "overstuffed" furniture. Wing chairs popular, loveseats developed to accommodate ladies hoopskirts, also lowboys and the provincial Windsor chairs. Splat-backed chairs and cabriole legs with duck, bun, hoof, or claw feet distinctive. Some carving, veneer, and lacquer work. Shell motif. Woods: walnut and some cherry.

ACCESSORIES

Tall clocks, silver candlesticks and boxes, Chinese porcelains, tapestries, mirrors, fire screens, brass and crystal chandeliers, Oriental, Aubusson, and needlework rugs.

COLORS AND FABRICS

Soft crimson, greens, blues, deep yellow, turquoise, off-white, gray. Crewel embroideries, hand-blocked linens, chintz with small foliage and flower designs, needlepoint, damasks, velvets, tapestries.

REMARKS

This style has long been one of the best loved in America. Wren and Grinling Gibbons were doing some of their best work at this time.

Early Georgian—1714 to 1754

ATMOSPHERE

"A heavy elaborately carved Queen Anne Style," with much emphasis on elaborate interior architectural detail. English

Renaissance architecture gave way to Georgian. Rich and ornamental.

FURNITURE CHARACTERISTICS AND WOODS

Elaborate carvings with acanthus leaf, eagle heads, lion heads, satyr mask, and shell motifs. Heavy cabriole legs with ball and claw feet. Pierced back splats; casters first in use. Woods: walnut and mahogany.

ACCESSORIES

Elaborate clocks, candlesticks, urns, Chinese vases, mirrors, crystal chandeliers, Oriental rugs.

COLORS AND FABRICS

Full-bodied crimson, greens, blues, and yellows. Single-color rooms appeared for the first time. These were red rooms, blue rooms, etc. Tapestries, velvets, mohairs, damasks, satins, brocatelles, printed linens, and chintz.

REMARKS

With the death of Wren, William Kent became the number one architect and furniture designer. To him was attributed most of the worst and some of the best furniture of the day.

Chippendale—1754 to 1779

ATMOSPHERE

Rich, graceful, refined, solid, basically English forms with three major styles influencing the embellishments—Gothic, Chinese, and most important, French Louis XV rococo, which was the forerunner of English Victorian.

FURNITURE CHARACTERISTICS AND WOODS

The work of Thomas Chippendale, the famous cabinetmaker, dominant; it was imitated and interpreted everywhere. His most distinctive characteristics appeared on chairs, which had flared backs, much carving—particularly fretwork and grooving in C and S scrolls, shell, ribbon, pagoda top, pierced splat and lattice motifs, straight Chinese or cabriole legs with ball and claw feet. Some "Chinese" pieces were lacquered. Woods: mahogany.

ACCESSORIES

Candlestands, clocks, fire screens, lanterns, pier glasses, brass candlesticks, Chinese pottery, and very distinctive drawer pulls and escutcheons.

COLORS AND FABRICS

Rich but muted reds, greens, turquoise, yellows, rose, mauves and grays. Printed English linens and French toiles de Jouy, damasks, chintzes, antique satins.

REMARKS

Chippendale was the first cabinetmaker to have a period named after him and probably the most famous of all time. He was born in the early 1700's but achieved prominence in 1754 when he published his book, *The Gentleman and Cabinet Maker's Director*.

Adam Brothers—1758 to 1794

ATMOSPHERE

Graceful, elegant. Classic influence: the Adam brothers, who were architects, studied in Italy and designed houses in the classic style. They then designed furniture to harmonize with it.

FURNITURE CHARACTERISTICS AND WOODS

Medium lightweight, rectilinear, angular, structural, carved and painted with classic motifs—wreaths, honeysuckle, fans, urns, lyres, medallions, rams' heads. Legs: tapered and decorated or round and fluted, spade or turned feet. Veneer and inlay. Woods: mahogany, satinwood, and harewood (sycamore dyed gray).

ACCESSORIES

Clocks, Wedgwood plaques, urns, candlesticks, Oriental rugs and Brussels carpets, oval hardware, gilt-framed mirrors, ormolu mounts introduced.

COLORS AND FABRICS

Soft grays, blues, mauves, yellows, corals, gilt and white, also a green called "Adam green." Smooth, rich fabrics with delicate designs: damasks, satins, linens.

REMARKS

The Adam brothers, often referred to as the Adelphi, from the Greek word meaning brothers, only *designed* furniture. The great cabinetworkers of the day interpreted the designs.

Hepplewhite—1762 to 1786

ATMOSPHERE

Graceful, elegant, classic. Adam brothers influence.

FURNITURE CHARACTERISTICS AND WOODS

Curvilinear, slender, and dainty, but strong. Carving, inlay, and veneer ornamentation. Most significant motif, three Prince of Wales plumes, also ears of wheat, lyres, and other classical motifs. Chair backs: shields, ovals, hoops and splats. Legs: straight and tapered most significant, also round, fluted, reeded. Spade foot. Serpentine front sideboards. Woods: satinwood, mahogany, rosewood, and fruitwoods.

ACCESSORIES

Mirrors, clocks, vases, candlesticks, fine potteries and porcelains, Oriental and Brussels carpets. Distinctive beaded oval hardware. Chinese objets d'art. Sconces.

COLORS AND FABRICS

Soft gray-greens, blue-greens, green-blues, pale yellows, buffs, and rose. Silks and satins with narrow stripes, linens, chintz, damasks; horsehair stuffing introduced.

REMARKS

When Hepplewhite died, his wife continued his business and two years later published his book, *The Cabinet-Maker and Upholsterers Guide.*

Sheraton—1780 to 1806

ATMOSPHERE

Refined, graceful. At its beginning, the Sheraton style was the epitome of classic simple elegance. Later pieces had many of the bizarre, vulgar extremes of French Empire.

FURNITURE CHARACTERISTICS AND WOODS

Similar to Hepplewhite but vertical lines emphasized. Slender, lightweight, beautiful inlay, rectangular chair backs. Straight, fluted legs, square or turned. Motifs: rosettes, urns, sunbursts, vases, lyres, stars, and swags. Disguised furniture introduced, twin beds, kidney-shaped pieces. Woods: mahogany, satinwood, and exotic veneering woods.

ACCESSORIES

Mirrors with characteristic frames having a frieze across the top, vases, clocks, candlesticks, Chinese objets d'art, porcelain plaques on furniture, distinctive drawer pulls having a ring in a lion's mouth. Oriental and Brussels carpets.

COLORS AND FABRICS

Soft colors: blue the favorite; blue and white, blue and black, blue and yellow. Striped and flowered silks, brocades, chintzes, toiles, knotted fringe.

REMARKS

Sheraton, too, wrote several books on cabinet design. His most famous, *The Cabinet-Maker and Upholsterers Drawing Book*, served as a guide for many.

English Regency—1795 to 1837

ATMOSPHERE

Refined, sometimes affected. The style was mainly influenced by the French Directoire and Empire styles, and in turn by the ancient Greeks, Romans, and Egyptians.

FURNITURE CHARACTERISTICS AND WOODS

Straight and Greek curved lines. Medium weight, more comfortable than the French counterpart. Straight or splayed legs, some spiral turned. Carved, veneered, and lacquered ornamentation. Cornucopias, honeysuckle, and Chinese and Egyptian motifs; wire grilles significant, also rolled-armed sofas, some caning. Woods: mahogany and rosewood.

ACCESSORIES

Clocks, candlesticks, Chinese art objects, paintings, etchings and prints. Oriental rugs and black and white marble floors significant.

COLORS AND FABRICS

Deep contrasting colors: reds, browns, gilt, also bright yellow, Chinese pink, lavender, salmon. Boldly striped damasks, satins, brocades and velvets.

REMARKS

This, in reality English Empire, had a classic charm and dignity in the beginning, but as it merged into Victorian, became clumsy and awkward.

Victorian—1837 to 1900

ATMOSPHERE

An eclectic style similar to the French and American counterparts. Unfortunately, pride in workmanship deteriorated with the machine age, so there were some quite bad pieces. Louis

XV and Egyptian styles most influential. Charles Eastlake and William Morris, both designers, made significant contributions to the period.

FURNITURE CHARACTERISTICS AND WOODS

Gingerbread ornamentation, low writhing lines and heavy carving. Motifs: fruits, flowers, leaves, scrolls; pressed gilt ornaments applied to furniture. Mother-of-pearl inlay and many marble tops. Woods: black walnut, mahogany, ebony, rosewood.

ACCESSORIES

Gilded pressed-metal ornaments, much silver plate, bric-a-brac, daguerreotypes, antimacassars, elaborate chandeliers and sconces (some with gas jets), artificial flowers in glass domes, many prints.

COLORS AND FABRICS

Harsh reds, dark greens (new dyes faded quickly), gilt, dark woods. Horsehair and plush, velours, velvets and charming nosegay chintzes.

REMARKS

Chippendale's French rococo style was actually the forerunner of the major elements of this period. One of the most creditable achievements of this period were the charming chintzes produced.

UNITED STATES

Early American—1607 to 1700

ATMOSPHERE AND ORIGIN

Early American and Colonial styles were simple adaptations of the ideas and articles (provincial cottage type) brought by the settlers from their homelands. Broadly these origins are: English in New England, Flemish in New York (which was similar to New England as England was copying Flemish styles), Spanish in Florida, New Mexico, and the West Coast, French in the South, Peasant Germany in Pennsylvania.
This, the earliest period, mainly concerns itself with copies of the English and Flemish styles.

FURNITURE CHARACTERISTICS AND WOODS

Simple, often crude adaptations of English styles—particularly Jacobean and William and Mary. The earliest styles were extremely straight-lined and simple—rush-seated side chairs with ladder or bannister backs typical. Later William and Mary trumpet-shaped legs, turnings, strapwork carving and applied and split spindles appeared. Motifs: Tudor rose, sunflower, scrolls, diamond shapes, circles, and pine trees. Trestle, gateleg and butterfly tables popular. Woods: pine, maple, cherry, oak, birch, and ash.

ACCESSORIES

Pewter cups, basins, tankards, candlesticks, etc. Wrought iron for fireplace equipment, hanging lanterns, etc. Guns, Bible boxes, copper cooking utensils, samplers, cradles, spinning wheels, sconces, rag and hooked rugs.

COLORS AND FABRICS

Warm reds, blues, greens, yellows, and browns against mellowed wood tones. Homespun woolens and worsteds, painted linens, chintzes, calicos, ginghams and fish nets, cretonne.

The terms Colonial and Early American are loosely used. Some writers use Colonial to denote furniture brought from abroad before the Georgian Era and Early American for pieces made here during the same period. Sometimes they are used interchangeably.

Colonial—1700 to 1781

ATMOSPHERE AND ORIGIN

A refined homelike atmosphere prevailed. This period is often referred to as American Georgian since the American styles were primarily copies of William and Mary, Queen Anne, Early Georgian, Chippendale, and Hepplewhite styles, which appeared in America almost as soon as in their homeland.

FURNITURE CHARACTERISTICS AND WOODS

Since most of the furniture of this period was English inspired, it had the characteristics of the English cabinetmakers it was patterned after. There was, also, the early painted Pennsylvania Dutch furniture, which showed regional adaptations and crude interpretations of copies of current styles from the homeland. Significant American contributions were general refinement and popularization of the spindle-backed Windsor chair in Philadelphia, the development of the rocking chair, generally attributed to Ben Franklin, and Goddard's and Townsend's New England blockfront furniture. Woods: usually hardwoods for formal furniture and softwoods for country.

ACCESSORIES

The accessories for the country farming people stayed much the same as those in the preceding period, but the wealthier classes were adding more and more luxuries to their homes, such as brass fireplace equipment, silver pieces, clocks (full clocks came in along with the wall and shelf clocks), mirrors, fine pottery and porcelain, engravings and botany prints. Hooked and braided rugs used in country. Oriental rugs popular in the cities.

COLORS AND FABRICS

White, cream, gray-blue, mustard, Georgian reds, greens, and browns. Cretonnes, chintzes, toiles de Jouy, damask, crewel embroideries, tapestries and needlepoint. The same home-spuns and ginghams of earlier period continued in farm homes.

REMARKS

America contributed some master craftsmen in this period. Among them were: William Savery, John Goddard, and John Townsend, cabinetmakers; the Willard family of Massachusetts, famous for their clocks; Paul Revere, silversmith; and Thomas Jefferson, who designed some handsome buildings. An American Spanish style, sometimes called Western Colonial, sometimes Monterey, had its beginning in 1769 and continued until 1850. This style employed driftwood finishes.

Federal—1781 to 1800

ATMOSPHERE AND ORIGIN

A refined lightweight and graceful blending of Adam, Hepplewhite, Sheraton, and French Directoire. In spite of the classic Greek revival in furniture styles, the character of the homes was much the same as that of the Colonial Period.

FURNITURE CHARACTERISTICS AND WOODS

It was in this period that Duncan Phyfe did his best work, following Sheraton lines. His distinctive characteristics were lovely, slender, graceful lines, splayed-footed pedestals for tables, sometimes reeded legs, dog's-paw and lion feet. His motifs were lyres, acanthus leaves, bunches of arrows, drapes, and swags. Eagles, stars, and pineapples were other motifs. Beautiful veneering. Woods: mahogany, some fruitwoods, particularly cherry and gum.

Candlesticks, clocks, Chinese porcelains, mirrors and giran-
doles (convex mirrors framed with lights), Sheraton mirrors,
paintings, etchings, and prints, brass sconces and chandeliers,
world globes, hooked and Oriental rugs.

COLORS AND FABRICS

Soft blues, grays, reds, browns, greens, and yellows. Damasks,
chintzes, toiles de Jouy, linens, haircloth, needlepoint, satins,
brocades, velvets.

REMARKS

This period (named after the Federation of States, which
America became after the Revolution had brought the
Colonial period to a close) grew quite naturally out of the
Colonial period—with America still following English and
European styles.

American Empire—1800 to 1825

ATMOSPHERE

A refined medium-heavy style based on the French Empire
style and combined with our Colonial style, with the classic
influence becoming Roman as well as Greek.

FURNITURE CHARACTERISTICS AND WOODS

The major furniture style much the same as French Empire
but with the addition of the American eagle everywhere, also
pineapples, stars, and the classic acanthus leaves, cornucopias,
and lyres. With the machine age came the Hitchcock factory,
which produced, partly by hand and partly by machine,
painted chairs with rush seats and stenciled backs along
Sheraton Empire lines. Spool furniture too was very popular.
Simple unadorned wooden knobs replaced metal pulls. Shaker
furniture flourished. Woods: mahogany, cherry, some maple.

ACCESSORIES

Clocks, cut-glass vases, Wedgwood-patterned candlesticks, paintings, etchings and prints, sconces, brass and crystal chandeliers, mirrors. Hooked and Oriental rugs.

COLORS AND FABRICS

Soft to rich reds, greens, blues, browns, tan, yellow. Damasks, chintzes, velvets, brocades.

REMARKS

Duncan Phyfe was still working, but his styles had deteriorated as a result of the demands of his clients.

American Victorian—1825 to 1900

ATMOSPHERE AND ORIGIN

A period with elaborate, ornate, and often exaggerated styles. Empire lingered for a while. By far the most popular theme was the revival of the French Louis XV style, which was taking France by storm. This style, with its exaggerated scrolled curves, was interpreted often by the leading cabinetmaker of the day, John Belter. There was also a Gothic theme in the early part of the period, and Charles Eastlake, an English designer, influenced the American scene shortly after the Civil War with his styles, which were mainly Empire in origin but showed traces of Jacobean. William Morris, proponent of the popular Morris chair, favored simple, direct styles. Italian Renaissance and Louis XVI styles were also in evidence.

FURNITURE CHARACTERISTICS AND WOODS

Overly ornate curves and embellishments. Heavy carving, with scrolls, foliage, pendants, and bunches of grapes the predominant motifs. Much jigsaw carving. Marble tops. Suites of furniture introduced. Tiffany glass, caned chairs, bentwood chairs—all quite popular today—were mid- to late-

Victorian. Woods: black walnut, red mahogany and rosewood. There was also a less formal style known as cottage furniture which included the spool, ball, and button-turned furniture, small drop-leaf tables, washstands, dry sinks and chests of drawers with wooden or iron pulls. These ordinarily were made of oak, pine, maple, or chestnut, but occasionally cherry or walnut, and were often painted either with solid colors, wood graining, or stenciling.

ACCESSORIES

Whatnots, blackamoors (statues in jet black), lithographs (Currier and Ives were of this period), steel engravings, charcoal portraits, antimacassars, hand-painted vases and lampshades for oil lamps, large floral patterned wallpaper, nests of tables, hassocks, ottomans, Axminster and Brussels carpets. Large pier glasses, porcelain figurines, silver-plated pieces, daguerreotypes, jardinieres. Pressed, mold-blown and cut glass. Ferns and palms much in evidence. In the country primitive art, painted tinware, pewter and wooden molds, wrought- and cast-iron implements and accessories were to be found.

COLORS AND FABRICS

Deep reds, maroons, greens, blues and browns. Velours, velvets, tapestries, haircloth, plush, needlework, all with lavish use of fringe, braid, and tassel trimmings. Tufted upholstery.

REMARKS

Until fairly recently the Victorian period was condemned as being grotesque, and furniture and accessories from this period were avoided like the plague by antique collectors. Recently, however, there has been a surge of interest in them, due in part to the scarcity of earlier pieces. This has made collectors turn their attention to the more plentiful Victorian pieces, which with the passing of considerable time since their original condemnation have come of age as antiques. The best pieces, in a proper setting, can be whimsical and charming.

Mission—1900 to 1910

ATMOSPHERE AND ORIGIN

Heavy, straightforward, and austere, originated on the Pacific Coast and had its inspiration in the Catholic missions in California.

FURNITURE CHARACTERISTICS AND WOODS

Massive, straight lines, with some scrolls, leather upholstery, iron and copper hardware. Woods: oak with a fumed or weathered finish (a decidedly more attractive one than the yellow oak finish being used elsewhere at the time).

ACCESSORIES

Accessories were in keeping with the style and were of iron, leather, and deep-toned pottery.

COLORS AND FABRICS

Deep tones of browns, reds and greens.

REMARKS

This style, one of many at the turn of the century, was the most significant. Its forerunner was the Spanish style, called Western Colonial or Monterey, 1769–1850.

INDEX